REWRITING

How MS Woke Me Up to the Life I Was Meant to Ride

CATE GREEN
FOREWORD MERRYL BLAIR

Copyright © 2025
First Published in Australia in 2025
By Morpheus Publishing PTY LTD
Geelong Victoria 3216
www.morpheuspublishing.com.au

ACN: 687 598 858 / ABN: 99687 598 858

All rights reserved. No part of this publication may be reproduced, stored in a retrieval system, or transmitted in any form or by any means, electronic, mechanical, photocopying, recording or otherwise, without the prior written permission of the publisher or author.

Paperback ISBN:	978-1-7641639-3-4
Author:	Cate Green
Editor:	Clare Reilly
Sub Editor:	Justine Martin
Cover Graphics:	Mylan Carascal

A catalogue record for this book is available from the National Library of Australia.

DISCLAIMER
The information contained in this book is for general informational purposes only. The author and publisher are not offering any medical, legal or professional advice. While every effort has been made to ensure the accuracy and completeness of the information provided, the author and publisher assume no responsibility for errors or omissions or any outcomes or consequences resulting from using this book's content.

COPYRIGHT
All original material in this book is the sole property of the author and Morpheus Publishing.

DISTRIBUTION
This book is distributed by Morpheus Publishing and is available through authorised distributors, booksellers, Morpheus Publishing website.

COPYRIGHT PERMISSIONS
For copyright permissions or any other inquiries, please contact:

PUBLISHER: Morpheus Publishing
www.morpheuspublishing.com.au |
hello@justinemartin.com.au | +61403 564 942 |

AUTHOR: Cate Green
https://www.morpheuspublishing.com.au/authors/cate-green

PUBLISHED WITH PURPOSE
Morpheus Publishing proudly supports this project.

This book, *Rewriting 2:33 – How MS Woke Me Up to the Life I Was Meant to Ride*, was published as part of Morpheus Publishing's Community Scholarship Program—an initiative dedicated to supporting voices that inspire change.

Morpheus Publishing donated all publishing services to help Cate share her incredible story and support her mission to raise funds and awareness for MS research.

This book is more than a memoir. It's a powerful reflection of resilience, hope, and the transformative journey of living with multiple sclerosis. Cate's next chapter is a bold one: a solo pushbike ride around Australia to raise money for MS research.

All profits from this book go directly towards funding Cate's national cycling journey and supporting life-changing MS research.

To follow Cate's ride or contribute to her fundraising efforts, please visit Morpheus Publishing's website www.morpheuspublishing.com.au or follow us on social media.

We are honoured to stand beside Cate as she rides for every person impacted by invisible illness.

Justine Martin CEO

**Morpheus Publishing —
Stories that shift the world.**

FOREWORD

Courageous...foolhardy...adventurous...insane... It can be hard to work out which adjective most suits Cate! I think I'd happily sit with 'heroic'; I'm sure all true heroes were a mixture of all of the above.

Why heroic?

I don't know too many people who would receive the diagnosis of a life-changing, degenerative disease with the determination to see just how far they can push their bodies. This is Cate's response, and she continues to find new frontiers to strive towards.

Those of us who have become addicted to her Facebook posts of her cycling journeys (Vietnam, the Camino de Santiago in Spain, her ride all around Victoria) know that she takes us on a life-changing journey with her; though for us, it all happens in the comfort of our homes (at my age, the best sort of adventure...But don't tell Cate I said that!).

Cate and her trusty bicycle, with or without the gorgeous canine companion Kobe, invites us into the stories of her days. These include disasters, unexpected meetings, getting lost, discovering unknown paths, and in general, closely observing the small and seemingly insignificant miracles of everyday life, as well as the scary and challenging times when MS reminds her that it is still very much part of her.

In these pages, we will encounter a wonderful travelogue as we see parts of Victoria via roads less travelled. We will also engage in conversation with Cate as she muses on what she is learning about life, the universe, and everything – especially her own response to living with MS. We will find an indomitable spirit, who faces economic uncertainty with a refusal to treat life with anything but gusto, while still being totally honest about the moments of despair.

Perhaps the greatest gift in reading this book, will be a renewed faith in the kindness of strangers. The lovely appearances, out of the blue, of generous and hospitable people, have constantly helped Cate's rides survive and move to the next phase. I, for one, find myself regularly moved and reassured that so much kindness still exists in our world. Cate's courage calls kindness forth, and I am sure these generous people feel amply rewarded by simply being part of her heroic journey. As will the reader: rewarded, enlightened, and encouraged to approach life with similar heroism.

Rev Dr Merryl L Blair

TABLE OF CONTENTS

Foreword v
Introduction 1
Why focus on disability? 5
Why name a bike? 9
Day One 11
Day Two 13
Day Three 16
Day Four 21
Day Five 24
Day Six 26
Day Seven 30
Day Eight 33
Day Nine 37
Day Ten 40
Day Eleven 45
Day Twelve 50
Day Thirteen 56

Day Fourteen	59
Day Fifteen	66
Day Sixteen	69
Day Seventeen	73
Day Eighteen	76
Day Nineteen	82
Day Twenty	88
Day Twenty-One	92
Day Twenty-Two	98
Day Twenty-Three	101
Day Twenty-Four	103
Day Twenty-Five	107
Day Twenty-Six	111
Day Twenty Seven	115
Day Twenty-Eight	119
Day Twenty-Nine	124
Day Thirty	126
Day Thirty-One	129
Postscript	133
What Is Multiple Sclerosis?	136

INTRODUCTION

My motivation to ride!

I was diagnosed with MS in September 2018. In hindsight it was a fairly mild 'relapse'. Although the physical symptoms subsided quickly, my mental health deteriorated as fear of what might be consume my every thought. I decided I needed something positive to focus on. An ad popped up on my Facebook feed about a fundraising cycling trip through Vietnam. I had liked cycling as a kid so figured I'd sign up. The ride was scheduled for March 2020. I had 18 months to prepare.

September 1, 2019 I woke to discover my left side of my body not working. I had an exhibition to prepare for, so I had no time for MS. I went to my GP and said, 'it's the wrong fucking week. We need to stop this now. I have 6 outfits to finish this week.' He told me rather 'flatly that he had no control over this disease but he would ring my neurologist to find what to do next.' I'm really good at denial, so I then said, 'well can I go back to work until then?' Stating the obvious, he replied,' as your left arm is not working, I don't see how that will be possible.'

I obeyed and headed home. On the drive home, I was heading over a railway bridge near my home. As I reached the crest of this bridge, my car suddenly slowed to 35 kms per hr. I swore at my car. The last thing I needed now was for my car to break down. However, I quickly realized that it wasn't my car that was the issue. I could no longer feel either of my feet. Miraculously, I made it home, dragged myself inside and called my GP. I told him I had a minor issue - both my legs had stopped working. He suggested that this wasn't minor and he'd ring the hospital ASAP. Turns out my neurologist was on the other side of the world attending a conference. My hometown hospital doesn't have a neurologist, so for the next 24 hours it was a battle to get someone to make a decision about the best way forward.

By the next night, my GP suggested I keep my phone by my bed just in case I needed to call an ambulance but otherwise he'd get me admitted to the local hospital in the morning. I woke up at 2:33am and couldn't move my legs or left arm at all. It was time to call 000 and my awesome neighbour, Krystal. By the time I arrived at the hospital, I couldn't move all four limbs. When I arrived, I started shaking uncontrollably. No one knew what to do other than keep me warm and hope it would settle.

I was admitted to a ward and then my bowel and bladder function stopped. I went into severe fits. I was given some drugs, given an MRI, but told they couldn't find a reason for my deterioration. I didn't improve with drugs, although the fitting subsided, I still couldn't move or go to the toilet. I spent 3 weeks in hospital learning to walk, use a toilet, use cutlery, and generally function independently again. One of the scariest moments was lying face down in a pillow one night unable to move arms or legs and not being able to breathe. I couldn't roll over by myself so yelling out to a nurse was my only option. The memory of nurses moving me, feeding me, toileting and showering me lingers still to this day. The feeling of being completely helpless is one of the most fearful things, I believe, an adult can face.

One of the challenges of MS is that there is never any guarantee of recovery when one 'relapses'. So rehab was my best (& really only) option for a chance of full recovery.

At the time, I had the immediate goal of riding through Vietnam on my bike, so my motivation to walk again was high. I spent 3 weeks in hospital and 4 months in outpatient rehab. On the six month anniversary of paralysis, I boarded a plane to Vietnam and then rode from the north to the south of Vietnam with 17 others raising money and awareness for MS Australia. I arrived home the day Australia shut its borders due to COVID 19. However, my love of cycling had been ignited and I spent most of lockdown on my bike improving my fitness and falling in love with the outdoors.

- Cate Green

WHY FOCUS ON DISABILITY?

Why focus on disability?

Annie's coming out.

My first encounter with 'disability' that changed the way I see the world.

The year was 1984 and I was 18 years old. It was just at the beginning of the push to integrate the disabled into mainstream society. A young couple turned up at church with four kids in wheelchairs from five to thirteen years old. One of the girls (Tina) had starred in a recent film called 'Annie's Coming Out' - a film about the deinstitutionalisation of the disabled. Tina had severe cerebral palsy. It was the first time I had encountered such profound disability

Eventually the young couple asked for volunteers to take Tina and one of the boys, John, to an able bodied camp. My parents had instilled in me deep compassion for the underprivileged, so I eagerly offered to volunteer, having no idea what I was getting myself into.

The camp was a hoot. In hindsight, we probably did some incredibly dangerous things but Tina and I had a great time.

Once home I continued to volunteer at the house to give Kim Ray and Geraldine a break. It was hard work but rewarding; however, I couldn't help but wonder whether we were merely overlaying our own ideas and desires onto these kids. Did they really comprehend what was going on?

Then one day Kim Ray and I took Tina and John into the city for the day by train. We pushed them through department stores, down streets and had a great time. At lunchtime, we couldn't find a table inside that could accommodate 2 wheelchairs so we sat on a bench in the street and fed Tina and John their lunch. It was a fairly messy affair. A woman stood nearby and stared. Tears came to her eyes as Kim Ray spoke to her and shared stories. She eventually went on her way.

We caught a train home and amazingly the same woman was on the same carriage. She smiled and sat a little way off and tried not to stare. Her station came up and as she got off the train she came and gave Tina $5. I thought it was a lovely gesture. Once the train started off again Tina grew very agitated, yelling and throwing her arms around. I pulled out of her communication board and started to point to words trying to understand what was wrong. I will never forget her sentence:

'She was angry with this woman because the woman would never give five dollars to a 'normal' child'

It entirely sealed in my mind that Tina knew exactly what what's going on and wanted to be treated the same as everyone else, like we all do. It was a harsh lesson in why we should never judge and also why 'special consideration' needs to be delicately handled.

Fast forward 40 years and I get introduced to the whole realm of 'invisible' disability. How does one integrate into society when there are no physical or visual signals that 'special consideration' needs to be given. I actually loathe the term 'special consideration' because like Tina, I just want to be treated like normal. But the reality is both Tina and those with invisible disability need some extra assistance to reach our goals. As Temple Grandin says, 'We are not less, we are different.'

A lifetime of listening to stories, assisting those with disabilities, and now living with one has given me a passion to raise awareness and create systems that can help those within invisible disabilities reach their full potential. It is the reason that 'Help me Mind my Own Business' was born.

- Cate Green

WHY NAME A BIKE?

Why (Bath)sheba?

I always name my bikes. My usual response when asked, 'Why do I name my bikes?' is; If something/one is going to be between my legs for an extended time I need to be on a first name basis.

However the names I choose are very intentional. My previous bike was called David. The reason was I purchased him when I had just returned from Vietnam and conquered my own 'Goliath' – the Hi-Van pass. So David seemed an apt name – My bike helps me conquer what seems, to the human mind, impossible.

This bike is named after David's wife – Bathsheba and there is a very specific reason. The story of David and Goliath is commonly understood – small guy defeats giant. But in the longer story of David, David has some very undesirable traits. His spots a woman bathing, he wants her, sleeps with her, gets her pregnant and then quietly gets the husband killed and then marries her. The resulting child dies but the marriage produces a child who then becomes the wisest man who has ever lived.

In the story, Bathsheba never speaks. Her opinion and feelings are never voiced. We can overlay our own version of what she may or may not have felt but we will never truly know. I have a passion for giving opportunities for the voiceless to be heard. My rides are about gathering stories of those who have 'invisible disabilities' and feel unsupported or not seen and therefore not heard.

In ancient times, the men got to tell the stories. In modern times, we often acquiesce and let the experts tell and interpret the stories of disability. Whilst statistics, research and expert analysis are needed, the lived experience of individuals are a powerful tool to not only self-empowerment but also to allow the uniqueness of each person to be seen and heard within their community and hopefully enable awareness which will lead to more kindness and support. Naming my bike Sheeba is therefore a statement that my ride is about giving voice to those who feel and believe they have none. Hopefully like the end of the original Bathsheba story, what will be birthed is a greater wisdom in how invisible disabilities are both perceived and treated within society.

DAY ONE

Sometimes the bravest step is the first one out the door—even when your whole body says no.

Day One PM

Eaglehawk to Dunnolly

Apart from a cold head and cross wind, it was a pleasant ride.

My gifts of the day:

A great send off at the Courthouse hotel in Eaglehawk. Loz, the Barista from the hotel has given me free coffee and toasties for the year as I've trained for this ride. I figured then it was fitting to start my ride from the hotel and invite friends and supporters to wave me goodbye. My bicycle coach (Tasman) and Exercise Physiologist (Tom) were there to wish me well. Tas even rode the first 12 kms with me to help settle the nerves. 28 days of solitary riding whilst exciting was also terrifying. The constant nagging fear of 'what happens if I wake up paralyzed', while no longer debilitating, does get louder when out in the bush miles from anywhere! So after a second coffee break at Marong, I was finally on my own.

I stopped at Newbridge for a cup of tea and a snack. I went to pay and the lady got distracted and walked away. I sat down, drank my tea, went back to pay, she took my money, but then handed it back to me. Unsure of reason but free morning tea was greatly appreciated! (It proved to be indicative of the generosity of the entire ride)

I arrived in Dunnolly early afternoon. I enjoyed a great evening with a friend, sharing stories, eating pizza and eventually falling into bed ready for the next day's adventure.

DAY TWO

When your world is spinning, find one truth to hold onto—and ride with it.

Day Two AM

I slept in a 'boat' last night in the backyard of a property in inland Victoria. The 'boat' has been redecorated into a Bohemian bedroom, the door is a 'magic' carpet and the windows, creative mosaics of broken glass. The bed was so cosy and comfy. The history of this boat is that it was a coral sightseeing boat with a glass bottom but it sank at one point, was rescued and transported to Airlie Beach Queensland. It eventually was transported (by very creative means) to the backyard of my friend's house and made into the most divine sanctuary of rest and restoration.

Last night I sat around the kitchen table eating pizza and sharing stories. I fell into bed content with the day's events, grateful for friends and a bed. I'd also had a conversation with a guy about why I am doing this ride. I can shrink the 'why' into three reasons:

1. Personal achievement. Every September I do some challenge to celebrate my body's ability to function.
2. Raising awareness of invisible illnesses and their impact on daily existence – especially one's ability to earn an income.

3. Raise money for MS Plus who provides support services for people with MS.

I often use pictures on cards as prompts for self reflection and writing. I randomly chose eight cards before I left home two for each week I was away. Week one's card was a mermaid in a broken boat and three mermaids on dolphins swimming to rescue the sinking mermaid.

This morning as I woke up in my 'boat that had sunk', I saw the relevance of the picture. MS plus Covid sank my 'lifeboat'. I lost my source of income (my business) due to the ramifications of life with MS. I saw no hope of recovery but like my friend's ability to decorate her sunken boat into a Haven of beauty and renewal, my life is being redecorated by my vision of what life can be.

I've been blessed with amazing 'mermaids on dolphins' who have helped rescue and rebuild my life (Team Cate and friends). It's still a work in progress but it's not a solitary project. I ride alone with the support of many behind me. It's what life in general must be but especially those living with chronic illness who often feel like they're living on a sinking ship.

Day Two PM 47 kms total

Sheeba and I are learning to negotiate crosswinds given her extra weight on her rear end. The morning's ride was filled with cold cross winds despite the sun being out and the scenery glorious. We finally came to some agreement and while exhausting, the rhythm of the ride fell into place. More frequent stops to replenish lost energy but we only had 47 km to do today.

Then suddenly I heard a truck approaching. I braced myself for the wind tunnel that such encounters create. But the sheep truck came so close, it blew Sheeba and I off the road. We stayed upright and no one was injured but it did scare me spitless.

As we continued, I was more alert to the surroundings. If we heard a truck, we stopped, waited and then continued. I figured slow and alive was better than fast and dead!

We arrived in Avoca, had lunch, set up my tent and went for a sightseeing ride minus Sheeba's extra weight. It's difficult to get out of 'training mode' and just enjoy the scenery but I'm getting there.

DAY THREE

When your world is spinning, find one truth to hold onto—and ride with it.

Day Three AM

Is this an MS hug?

Two systems that perpetually 'fail' for me are pain and temperature regulation because of a faulty central nervous system. I can either experience pain when I have no 'physical' reason to or I feel no pain when I have every physical reason to. In terms of temperature I can feel cold when the ambient temperature is warm and vice versa.

So last night as I crawled into my tent, my chest started to feel really tight. I've been taught a checklist to avoid panic. The pain feels like heart issues, but I know my heart is healthy, (I've had it checked). So my options were this- An MS hug or anxiety? I have no control over an MS hug but I do over anxiety. Again I've been taught management skills so with some simple breathing exercises the pain subsided.

I then realised I was cold but my checklist - warm clothes, sleeping bag, socks, tent all indicated that my central nervous system was misfiring so I could relax and suddenly I was warm. My arms and shoulders ached. Again there was a rational reason. I had braced myself against the wind for the whole day. So similarly, I knew this would pass and happily fell asleep.

However, the more difficult task is when I feel nothing. What I had believed to be a 'high pain threshold' was merely a misfiring nervous system and I was 'traumatising' my body doing extraordinary things. There's a fine line between bravery and stupidity. Pushing the limits can be a good thing but also extremely idiotic. It's why I have 'Team Cate'. They've taught me methods of self regulation which largely involve reading external cues rather than purely internal (because the internal is unreliable). So I eat and drink after 45 minutes of exercise because normally I don't experience hunger or thirst. I rest on regular intervals, because sometimes I don't know if I'm tired. It may seem like an incredibly disciplined life but actually allows much freedom and safety. I'm out here on my own because I've been taught the skills to manage my condition. However, my team is still needed. Just last night I received a text from one member which simply said, 'Are you feeling okay?' My immediate response was, 'It's day two, of course I am' but it was also a prompt to remind me to check in with myself because 'naturally' I won't. I'll just keep going.

Emotional regulation is the same. Self regulation is a key topic at present. I also have an overzealous emotional system or one that feels nothing. The overzealous part I've been taught to self regulate using external cues. However, the feeling of nothing can also lead to bravery or stupidity. In my tent last night between two caravans of single men, I was struck by the thought, 'Is this brave or stupid? I figured it was brave and happily went to sleep but there have been other times when I put myself in relationships that are extremely unsafe because I feel no danger. My emotional regulator got broken a very long time ago and I've had years of learning skills to regulate them, but I also have people around to help me remind me of danger when the system is overloaded.

We would never get angry at someone with low vision for using external support to maintain his independence. Neither should we get angry with people with 'invisible disabilities' for using external support for emotional, pain or temperature regulation. I largely live an independent life but do it with a lot of support. Personal responsibility plus community/professional support leads to an awesome life.

Day Three PM

I dislike the wind (& criticism) or so I thought...

Today was 60.4 kms of strong head and cross winds with no let up the whole way. To make matters worse, I had assumed that the town at the 30 km mark would have food and water, which when I got there, discovered that it didn't. I had plenty with me but it helps to manage my anxiety if I know I've got options. So telling myself I had enough to get me the extra 30 kms, I continued. But the next 30 km was spent tackling not only head winds but also negative self-talk that I 'should' be more prepared. I should've listened to my coach better. I was extremely harsh on myself. The reality was though, that I did have enough. It was my expectation that had been 'faulty'.

I swore at the wind. I 'talked' to the wind asking what its purpose was other than to make my life miserable. I decided I hated wind! But then, for a brief moment, I caught a tail wind, and I instinctively said, 'Now that's better'. But the wind 'spoke' back- 'Ah you like me now!'

My response as always was 'Why?' The answer was easy - it was assisting me, which then led me to thinking about my journey of recovery, about learning to ask for help. To ask for help, one first has to admit they can't do something. And then they have to be willing to be helped or taught how to do said task.

At heart, I am a perfectionist. I don't like 'not being good at something'. So asking for help is extremely challenging. I like learning though. But I hate criticism or so I thought until the wind changed direction yesterday.

Wind is like criticism, it depends on the direction from which it comes as to whether it's helpful or harmful. I have a team that has taught me new ways of being which have been highly uncomfortable. A recent experience was when Rob asked me to dance my routine on my own. I was so uncomfortable. I knew I didn't know it well enough and feared the criticism. He reframed the experience as 'knowing where I needed help!' From learning to stand to learning how to get on my bike, I found I was 'doing it wrong' but therapists never framed it that way. They would say, 'There's a safer, more efficient, effective way' All I 'heard' was I was doing it wrong.

I think the reason was because my experience of criticism in my past has been delivered as a 'headwind' - a harsh delivery of 'you should change direction. Today, I was quite tempted numerous times to turn around and go back to Avoca because I knew I'd have a tail wind. Life would be so much easier. Sometimes, criticism seems harsh because others (or even your inner critic) believe you 'should' be heading in a different direction. Yet you are convinced of your destination.

My experience of my current team is that their 'criticism' (or rather feedback) is to help me achieve my desired destination/goal. (They are my tail wind) Whereas, others have believed that I should be heading back to my old life, where it's 'easier'. A previous EP said to me once, 'It would be easier for us if you stayed in front of your sewing machine or piano. However, you want to do all this crazy stuff, so our job is to make it as safe, effective amd efficient as possible.' Knowing that they believed in my vision, trusted my judgment, made the learning experience so much easier. We can laugh at my 'mistakes' and let go of the need to be 'perfect'

Collaboration in the journey of life is so healthy. Pre Prescribed destinations and routes are often 'easier' but often do not bring about the life enhancing qualities that collaboration brings.

Letting go of my business, letting go of 'old ways of being' has been so difficult. Sometimes because it's what I've loved and sometimes because it's easier. It's what I know. However, I have discovered that when being assisted by a 'tailwind' of feedback and support, the horizon of hope for a better future becomes tantalizingly bright.

DAY FOUR

Healing isn't passive—it's the work of listening inward, again and again.

Day Four

The Winds of change.

More wind stories.

Last night I went to a seminar put on by 'Pain Revolution'. My friend (and OT) Nikki had invited me. We stayed in the cabin and ate well. I learned heaps. Two highlights – the language we use around pain impacts how we experience it and a really weird 'illusion experiment' that kinda freaked me out. But the greatest takeaway was one of 'mindset'.

So this morning when I looked at the weather map and saw winds predicted at 30 km with gusts at 60+ kilometres an hour I began to panic. I couldn't cope with another day like yesterday. But then I thought of the lesson learnt last night. What if I changed my mindset? I survived yesterday. I've eaten and slept well. There was no reason to panic. I advised a Plan B just in case. I break down my days into 15 km sections. My original plan was 75 kms. That's 5×15 km. I do one at a time and reassess. So after a delightful breakfast with Nikki, I headed off towards Dunkeld. Although bitterly cold, the wind was mild and I had this day nailed.

But as the weather app had predicted, on the dot of 10 am the wind picked up. Rather than fight it, I took a different approach and here's what I learnt:

1) Sheeba and I are now well acquainted with our extra baggage. We work well together and so my confidence in getting off the road onto gravel and grass when trucks pass has greatly increased. Hence, I feel a lot safer. Similarly, like I learnt last night, when body and mind cooperate with each other, despite their limitations, one can achieve great things.

2) Reading the landscape. Open fields, while pretty, are nightmarish for wind. With no protection it's merely a case of head down, keep pedaling, and brace yourself. Whereas sections where trees lined the road were places I could relax a little or if need be, stop and refuel. Following on from my theme of wind and criticism, reading the landscape became a metaphor for reading people. Some of the criticism (headwinds) that come my way come from good intent. However, sometimes people's mode of delivery of criticism seems harsh. I don't need to fight it, just keep my head down and keep pedaling. But the trees are my friends/support that help buffer the harshness of those 'winds' so I can relax and replenish my energy reserves.

So with a much more relaxed attitude towards wind today (and some swearing) I arrived in Willaura to contemplate; 'Do I continue or call it a day. The advice from locals (and my coach) was to call it a day. So I did! I stocked up on food and supplies, found the campsite and began to relax.

But the sun came out andI began to think I could tackle another 15 or 20 km. Soaking in the sun seemed indulgent.

But then the wind would change and remind me of its unpredictability. Eventually, I surrendered to the idea that rest was actually okay.

The weather is supposed to be the same tomorrow but if I leave early enough, I may get a couple of hours of gentle winds. I am ever the optimist.

DAY FIVE

You don't have to be whole to move forward—you just have to believe it's worth it.

Day Five AM

Why is there no wind?

Being in the middle of nowhere, when it got dark, I crawled into my tent, read for a bit and promptly fell asleep. I woke feeling refreshed but was unsure of the time. I found my phone – 2:40 am.

When I was released from hospital five years ago, for months afterwards, I used to wake up at 2:33 am to check that all four limbs were working. It was the time I had woken to find I couldn't move. I had to retrain my brain that I was fine, that I could sleep through the night and trust my body would be ok. But every now and then if I'm in unfamiliar surroundings, my body remembers and will wake. So 2:40 am wasn't surprising last night.

As I lay in my tent, I listened to the outside sounds. It was completely still – no wind. An occasional truck in the distance, but other than that, silence. My thought, Why is there no wind? (Also, why can't I ride right now?) I realised I was tense 'waiting for the wind'. But (as you do at 2 am) I began to realise I spend most of my life 'waiting for the wind' - I am hyper vigilant for anything negative, ready to fight it off or brace myself, especially when it's dark.

In a society obsessed with positivity, it's a given that we banish all negative thoughts. In my case, my hypervigilance springs from the fear of darkness – depression. The darker emotions- grief, loss, sadness and anger are to be avoided for fear that they'll lead down dangerous roads to catastrophising or worse still suicidal tendencies. But last night as I lay in complete darkness and stillness, I wondered, 'can I relax in (even enjoy) the darkness?' 'Can I experience grief without fear?'

It took awhile but I went through some body scan exercises, and other relaxation techniques and fell into the deepest sleep I've had in ages. I woke to the sun rising ready to face the day whether that involves sunshine, wind or rain. I know I can trust my body and mind to deal with any scenario, just like Sheeba and I have learnt to trust each other.

Day Five PM

Today would have to be the most brutal riding I've ever done in all my years of cycling! Winds, rain and even hail. There were some brief reprieves but overall 70 kms of brutality! I sent my coach a photo of the conditions - me stranded on the side of the road in bushes while it poured with rain and the trees bent in the wind. His response: 'Think of it as good for resilience!' My thought: 'Fuck resilence!' I think I deserve a rest day tomorrow! I'm staying in a real house tonight with a real bed! So I'll sleep very well!

DAY SIX

Recovery isn't linear, and resilience doesn't mean you never pause. It means you return wiser.

Day Six

A day of rest: whatever that means!

I enjoyed a meal at the pub last night thanks to a friend back home. The taxi driver who took me there told me if I wanted to do some sightseeing there were two nice waterfalls just out of town that were worth seeing. He initially said they were 20 km out of town but then changed and said, 'No I think it's a 20 kilometres round-trip'.

Now, as I got out of the taxi, my mind went into 'definition' mode - 20 km of riding would qualify as a rest day surely but 40 km definitely wouldn't. By the time I got home later that evening the exhaustion of the day had set in (but I still wanted to see the waterfalls).

I began to feel incredibly nauseous. My body doesn't communicate 'pain' conventionally. I have learnt that nausea, for me, means I'm in a lot of pain, because I'm not hearing the subtler cues it gives. So my body says, 'Okay, I will make you throw up and then you'll listen!' So recognising it's screams for rest, I fell into bed and slept soundly. I slept in and woke to a house filled with light. The very first thing I do in the morning is check my legs are working. They were. The temptation was then, 'Are they working enough to ride to the waterfalls? Now when my enthusiasm for life exceeds rationality, I ask, 'what would my team say in such a scenario?' The answer was glaringly obvious – a 40 to 50 km ride does not constitute rest.

So I made a cuppa and researched other ways of getting to the falls but no clues. So my only option is to 'randomly' meet someone today who's heading that way. The chances are slight but one never knows.

Rest for me is hard. The concept of doing nothing is scary. Boredom is 'bad' for me. So as I sat in bed with my tea contemplating how I would fill my day. I noticed the more subtle cues of pain in my legs- very mild pins and needles in my entire legs. I was still in pain. It's just my body's communication skills are not 'normal'. I've had to learn its language.

It's the same in all relationships. Words (and experiences) mean different things to different people. Rest is boredom for me but to others it's delightful. Riding 20 km is relaxing for me, others find it damn hard work. Neither of us are right or wrong but rather the question is 'do those definitions bring life to each of us?' Today my definition of rest certainly will not bring life. 20 kilometres today will impede my chances of continuing the bigger ride tomorrow.

Learning new definitions, new ways of communicating with both one's body and others is challenging, but ultimately when we do it leads to a much healthier and fulfilling existence.

Day Six Lunchtime

My version of rest

So after breakfast I rode into the info centre (about 3 kilometres) to see if there was another way of getting to the falls. There wasn't but the brochure said that one of them was only 5 km out of Hamilton. One is better than none and 10 km is 'allowable' I thought. But when I put the address into 'Komoot', it chose a 16. 3 km route. Not one to take 'No!' easily, I tried Strava. It chose a 12.3 km route. I finally had to admit defeat. But I saw a sign to the train station. Maybe if I caught a train to Portland tomorrow that would count as my rest day and I could see both falls today. But alas, no trains, only buses and not till Monday. Sheeba doesn't like buses so I had to submit to the idea of rest.

I took a different route home and stumbled upon the Botanic Gardens. I took out my camera and we (Sheeba and I) wandered around. I love ducks. So we started at the pond. We then discovered an aviary. We couldn't enter but my camera can photograph through wire so I spent ages just watching and capturing moments. Photography is my form of meditation. Time stands still and my brain stops.

Eventually we found our way back to the gate and decided a late morning tea was in order. A short ride back to where I'm staying (via a Lake) and I was content to curl up on the couch for the rest of the day. Sometimes if we let go of our intentions, better ones show up. Bird photography was a much better option for me today.

I'm staying in a beautiful home of someone I have never met - a friend of a friend. I have the house to myself so relaxing on the couch wrapped in blankets drinking tea and editing photos is quite blissful. See, I can 'do nothing'.

DAY SEVEN

You don't have to carry everything alone—strength is found in being seen, supported, and loved.

Day Seven

The 'second time syndrome'. Learning to trust again

Hamilton to Portland

Today was a stunning ride but it didn't start that way. After a very relaxing day yesterday, I thought I better plan today's ride. The weather app said conditions were going to be similar to Friday's – strong westerly winds and rain. I began to panic. I decided to shorten the day to Haywood- 63 km.

I eventually went to sleep but woke early- every muscle in my body was complaining, my brain extremely anxious. I didn't think I could do another 70 km in wind and rain. Friday almost broke me. I couldn't do it again. I knew I didn't have an option so I wracked my mind for strategies to reframe.

I remember the section from Russell Nankervis book about a recent cycling adventure. He mentions that often we only remember the 10% of the day that was challenging and forget the 90% of the good. I revisited Friday memories. Nope! Russell's logic didn't work. 90% of the day was shit and 10% was good. But then I remembered most of the challenging parts I actually enjoyed the battle. It wasn't until the last 10 km when it started to hail and 50ft trees were bending in half in the wind and I was stuck in the bushes and lost I lost my will to ride. While I had reframed the day slightly, I still didn't want to ride today. Eventually, I just resigned myself to the day, did some 'box breathing' to calm the nerves and fell back asleep.

I left early, figuring the wind doesn't pick up till 10 am but it was drizzling. 'It is what it is' was my attitude. I put my feet in freezer bags to prevent them from freezing and started my day. After a few kilometres the sun came out. 'Komoot' had chosen a back route that was stunningly beautiful and protected from the wind. 25 km went in record time. The next 40 km was spent alternating between enjoying the sun and putting on my raincoat. I had morning tea in a cafe called 'The Stalkers Bend'. Not a very comforting name for a single woman. But nice coffee.

I arrived in Heywood by lunchtime. The weather turned nasty. Rather than panic, I ordered a 'second' lunch - doughnut and tea and waited till the storm passed. Then I made record time to Portland with enough daylight to take some photos.

The day reminded me how I don't like 'second time things' from paralysis to marriage to 2nd pregnancies to career changes. When one encounters hurt or trauma the first time, trusting that you'll cope a second time, let alone enjoy the experience requires courage. But today I realised I wasted a whole lot of worrying when I could've just trusted the process.

The added bonus of the day was I found a campsite which had a beautiful fire pit. While warming myself, I got chatting to the owners. They have offered to organize some fundraising event when I ride through here next year! Learning to enjoy the process pays off!

DAY EIGHT

Pain reminds us we're still alive, and purpose reminds us why we keep moving.

Day Eight

Equinoxes, new beginnings and F*ck I'm stuck!

Yesterday was the spring equinox here in Australia. I watched a YouTube clip on Saturday night on the 'spiritual' significance of equinoxes. Spring Equinoxes represent new beginnings. I thought that appropriate. Portland is where I change direction and in many ways feel like this is where I 'start' my trip.

As I rode yesterday, I'd hoped the campsite I chose would have a fire pit. A girlfriend and I always have 'witches fires' when we want to mark leaving the old behind and beginning something new. A fire seemed a good way to mark the equinox. So I was super excited when I arrived to find the fire already burning. A group of us sat around it last night sharing stories of travels, weather, bikes etc. I was content and happy when I crawled into my tent. I half stripped off once in my sleeping bag, I didn't want to get too hot. I wanted to wake up early to catch the sunrise, the beginning of a new chapter.

The danger of an over inflated sense of optimism is that it can slip into denial. I have a tendency to think of new beginnings as I'll beat MS and never have to struggle with symptoms again. You know: 'A positive mental attitude conquers all' belief system. However, denial never wins!

When I woke up this morning and rolled over my body flew into a 'clonus' attack. A mild version is tremors in my leg or arm. Full-blown it looks like I'm having a seizure. I know I'm not. It's just violent muscle spasms but for anyone looking on it looks like a medical emergency. I know the trigger is usually rapid change in temperature or being overtired. I was still toasty warm so it wasn't temperature related. So maybe I shouldn't have done that extra 26 km yesterday, was my thought. But hindsight is fairly useless to fix the present. Once the spasms subsided, I knew I couldn't move quickly or the scenario would repeat. But even small movements seemed to trigger a repeat performance. I lay there thinking, 'F*ck, I'm stuck!'

I really wanted to get to photograph the sunrise but I couldn't move. Also, calling for help seemed pointless - all I'll do is frighten them - observers of a half naked woman in seizure mode. This was NOT my vision of new beginnings. I wanted to will my way out of it but it wasn't going to happen that way today. Tension only makes it worse. I relented and figured I could at least get a couple of pics from my tent. I very slowly opened the flap enough to get my camera out. I feared the cold air would trigger another episode. I took a few photos and laid back. The tightness in my legs began to subside, the pins and needles lessened. Maybe, it was temperature related. Maybe I was just too hot. I cautiously opened the tent and my whole body relaxed. A new learning experience, but grateful for the reprieve.

I managed to shower and get to see the sunrise. My legs still felt a little dodgy but strong enough to get some riding in. The sunrise was stunning. Everything seems brighter, when you can risk losing everything. As I sat watching the sunrise, I wondered, what is my new beginning?

My answer: A new relationship with my body, I have an iron will and it has helped me achieve amazing things. It's not a bad characteristic. It is though, when it's used to manipulate and force others (including my body) to do as I wish. I see living with MS as a marriage relationship. Generally, I've been a 'control freak' within that marriage and not allowing my 'partner' to speak for fear it would be abusive. Yet today I learned if I listen I can avoid 'abuse' and gain rapid recovery. Mindset is 90% of a life with MS but it doesn't have to always be combative.

Sheeba, I discovered this morning, also has a lame leg. Her stand is stuck. So I needed to head to a bike shop and get her seen to before we see how many kilometres we could ride today.

A huge shout out to NRMA Caravan Park (Hamilton).

With my dodgy start to the day and the constant rain, I was struggling to get going. My tent pole bag blew away and as I went chasing it I ran into a guy with a golf buggy. We chatted, he worked at the park and his wife has MS. We chatted for ages and told him I had to go get my bike stand fixed. Instead, he said to take it down to the maintenance shed and he'd take a look. He did and Sheeba has her leg back! I set off slightly energized from such a gesture of kindness.

10 km down the road I get a message from the park saying I'd left my battery pack behind. The thought of riding back almost unglued me but I desperately need it. I couldn't ride back so messaged back to say just to leave it. But as I rode on, the anxiety of what if... scenarios raced through my mind. None of which were pretty. But I knew I was wasting energy on worry.

I resolved to just push pedals until I got to Port Fairy and 'worry' about it then. All of a sudden, a car stops just ahead of me and out jumps Dee (park manager) from the park with my battery pack! I could've hugged her (or cried). She took a chance to find me (there were multiple routes I could've taken).

Again the kindness energized me to keep pedaling. I found a coffee place down the road, refueled and continued my journey. I think I need to name this tour the 'don't panic tour!'

(Dee, thank you and there is coffee in Narrawong!)

DAY NINE

You are allowed to hurt. You are allowed to hope. You are allowed to hold both.

Day Nine

This is why I ride!

Random encounters.

Last night I arrived in Port Fairy utterly exhausted. I put up my tent and walked around the corner for takeaway, strolled up a short hill to look at the ocean and wandered back to eat dinner and fall into bed. As I was eating dinner, I posted some pics of my day. A response came up from a 'random person' on a 'random site' I've joined (worldwide) that said 'that's my parents place!' I responded, 'Ha! What are the chances'. Unbeknownst to her I had actually spoken to her parents. I pulled into the driveway because I needed a food break. I squatted by the fence under a pine tree and ate my banana when all of a sudden her mum drove out of the drive. She stopped and chatted and told me I was welcome to enjoy my banana. She drove off. Refueled, I got back on my bike and started to head out the driveway when another car pulled in. This time it was the dad. Again we chatted and I rode off.

I thought about the randomness of both encounters and then fell asleep. I woke early and started to pack up my stuff. I had not bought any milk on my way in the previous night, so I was eager for a coffee and my porridge. So as I packed my things I was tossing up between buying breakfast in town (costly in money but economical in energy) or buying milk and making my own (economical in money but costly in energy) then all of a sudden a runner ran to me, 'Hi I'm Emma from the cycling group. Are you Cate?' Surprised, I said, 'Yes'. We chatted and then she said, 'Do you want to come back to my place for coffee and breakfast. She had no idea of the dilemma I was wrestling with.

Her home was literally around the corner from where I camped and she taken a detour on her run this morning in the off chance she'd find me. I rode to her place. She cooked porridge, gave me coffee and toast and we shared stories. We discovered a random connection of a physio we both knew. Eventually, I said I'd better go. So she packed me a huge picnic of food to take with me. She also mentioned she could find me a bed for the night if I needed one. I had a Plan A but told her if that didn't come through, I'd call her. And then started my ride. 45 km for the day. I leisurely wove my way to Warrnambool taking photos along the way. 'This is why I ride', I told myself. Scenery, weather and new friends.

At lunchtime Plan A didn't eventuate so I messaged Em and asked for help. The result- A home with a piano, bath, bed and dinner all provided. Piano playing is the ultimate form of relaxation for me. I used to be a music teacher. I sat down and played. Emma was excited as the house had been her grandparents and her Pop was a piano tuner. My dad had been a pianist and pipe organist. So her Pop would've been very happy and so too my dad. Emma left me to enjoy the home by myself for the evening. I sat by the fire drinking tea eating a feast that was a pure gift.

The kindness of humanity always catches me off guard. But I am in awe of the randomness of human connection. In three days, I have gained three incredible friends and been provided for even before I could ask.

DAY TEN

This isn't just about kilometres—this is about reclaiming every part of you that was once doubted.

Day Ten AM

A day of rest – take two!

Being anxious about being anxious!

I woke this morning and reached out to open my tent and then suddenly remembered I was in a bed in a house. I smiled at the generosity of others making that possible. But today is my second rest day. Not something I'm good at. Emma had said there was no rush to leave this morning so as I lay in bed, I wondered if I could just stay in bed for the morning. It was grey outside. I've visited Warrnambool numerous times so sightseeing wasn't urgent. But merely sleeping seemed a 'waste' or 'indulgent', but the bed was super comfy.

A friend made a comment yesterday that kind of stuck with me:

'I hope you allow yourself the grace to congratulate yourself on a life very well lived'.

The concept was foreign to me. I wondered what that might look like.

As I lay in bed and did my usual 'body scan' to see if all body parts were functioning today. I thought I just wanted a day off from managing MS, from managing my mental health. I have often justified my vigilance for monitoring my symptoms/mood to that of a diabetic monitoring their blood sugar levels. If they don't, the consequences are dire.

But this morning I was challenged by the difference between vigilance and hyper vigilance. My default setting is to be anxious but shifting to 'being anxious about being anxious' takes it to a whole new level.

Journaling (and list making) are management skills for anxiety. It's like if I get it on paper I can leave it there and enjoy my day. So rather than get tied up in knots this morning over 'being anxious about being anxious' I lit the fire and decided I'd 'logically' deal with it so I could 'allow myself grace to congratulate myself'. Vigilance is merely my to-do list. Hyper vigilance a constant state of 'alertness'. So here is my 'logical' definitions:

Hyper:

>(Where)
>Have
>You
>Put
>Energy
>Reserves

Grace:

>Giving
>Rest

> Allowing
> Creative
> Energy

Initially, they looked the same but I wondered how to shift from one to the other.

My answer:

> Trust
> To
> Rest
> Understanding
> Surrender
> Triumphs

I'm not good at 'trusting' or 'surrendering'. Yet this ride is proving that trusting and not panicking is possible. I'm usually constantly asking 'what do I need to do next?' whether in terms of money, energy levels, symptom management and when it is appropriate to ask for help. Yet I've discovered amazing generosity without even asking. It's not wrong to ask, but when done from a place of anxiety it is detrimental to everyone's well-being.

So I decided that a small change was in order. I can't go from total anxiety to total surrender overnight. What small change can I make today to congratulate oneself and trust that all will be well?

Spending money is the most anxious thing I suffer from. Asking for it almost invokes panic attacks. The self loathing it evokes is scary. So reminiscing on the last few days I realised my needs were being met without the exchange of cash. But cash is surely needed, I thought. Can I surrender to the concept 'the universe will provide' without micromanaging what that will look like?

That was today's challenge. I made a big cup of coffee. (Em's husband had brought me milk last night on his way home from work). I sat back in front of the fire and made my essential to do list, check emails, pay bills, do nothing. The first email – a donation from a total stranger on my GoFundMe page. I laughed. I had not asked. I've made no plea for assistance and yet someone I don't know had taken the time to find a way to help with cash.

I am always amazed at the synchronicity, at random acts of kindness, whether the words, food, bed or money. Life is sheer gift. It's my definition of grace. It's not that we don't work, plan or 'be responsible' - that vigilance. But hypervigilance is a lack of trust in the goodness of life.

Today is a small step towards trusting. I can do nothing and my life won't fall apart.

I'll let you know how it goes....

Day Ten PM

So, I pushed myself out of my comfort zone in so many ways today! Firstly, I took a lazy morning, slept, played the piano and 'did nothing'. I had decided to catch the train to Camperdown today and follow the rail trail to Port Campbell tomorrow. Chatting with my coach yesterday, I realised that with a loaded bike and adverse conditions, 75 km is probably my daily limit. Warrnambool to Port Campbell was 90. So I surrendered to a change of plan and 'cheated' and caught a train part way. Besides, trains are 'resting' right?

I did a short ride to some familiar places in Warrnambool before hopping on the train. The wind was bitter so I was glad of a train ride. I watched out the window as the weather deteriorated. The thought of sleeping in a tent was terrifying.

I looked up the cost of a cabin but it was totally out of my reach. I'd received some money today unexpectedly but not enough to warrant splurging on a cabin! However, just as I pulled into Camperdown, I thought I'd check Booking.com for any other options. There was 1 hotel room available for precisely the amount I'd been given today. I booked it- so outside my comfort zone. To add to the blessing, I received a discount and breakfast. In total, I spent $30 more than a tent site!

As I settled in my luxury for the night, I received a message from a good friend. I told her of my splurge! Next thing I know, she donates the difference between a camp site and room with some left over for dessert! At which point I burst into tears!

'Undeserved Grace' is so hard to receive but thoroughly appreciated and so so healing!

DAY ELEVEN

Vulnerability and victory often ride side by side—keep going, even when it trembles.

Day Eleven AM

Escaping a life of Shame and Blame

I was talking to my coach the other day and told him I almost wanted to quit. He reminded me of my 'why'. When I first started training with Tas, he asked me for my why, why do I want to ride? His motto is:

If you have a strong enough why you'll put up with almost any how!

Why and how are my two most favourite questions in life. So I knew Tas would be a great team member.

Both in my journey of dance and cycling, personal development is part of my 'why' My dance journey has very much been about escaping a shame based existence. It's been wildly healing as I've learnt the 'how' of moving my body in sync with another body and keeping in time. My cycling journey I am discovering is about escaping a blame based existence and I'd like to explain why and how.

My journey towards freedom from a shame base really started when I understood the difference between shame and guilt. Brené Brown's definition of those words opened my eyes to how I interpret thoughts, feelings and experiences. As that foundation, dance became the method of learning new ways of being.

I've struggled with the concept of blame for years. A common theme in personal development circles is that you cannot blame anyone for your circumstances. You are responsible for your well-being. I hated the concept and it hooked into my shamed existence and drowned me in self loathing. There are very specific reasons for how I got to where I am today. Some of those reasons are external- people and institutions that have been abusive. Some are internal - how I have responded to that abuse. But I could never escape my desire for justice. I wanted accountability and that started with blame. Or so I thought.

Last night as I became overwhelmed by my sense of 'undeserved grace' on this ride, I started down the road of internal blame - all the reasons I didn't deserve to be treated so generously. Blame quickly turns to shame. And I've learned to recognise the prison chains of shame very quickly so I immediately paused.

Remembering the power of the definition of the word shame and guilt to enhance escaping a shame based existence I wondered if it would be the same with blame. I had assumed blame and reason were the same thing. They are not. Blame paralyses you in the past. Reasons promote movement towards a better future. So I came up with these definitions:

> Blame = B(e) lame
> Reason = It's just a season and seasons change.

Like in the natural world, climate change has led to unpredictable weather patterns, so too, a life with MS has led to unpredictable weather patterns - My mood and functionality can be highly unpredictable. Yet in both scenarios (climate change and MS) there is HOPE. Small changes make incremental differences and eventually that adds up to massive improvement. My journey to recovery (learning to walk/ride again) began with three minutes in a seat pushing pedals in a rehab ward and now five years later I'm cycling 70+ kilometres a day on my own.

Small change helps.

A cure for MS (and climate change) would be great but in the meantime I know the reason why my body and mind behaves the way they do. But the season will change. I just need to be patient and keep making small incremental changes to my lifestyle so I can enjoy each season whether that be the stormy wind or bright sunshine.

From my bedroom window this morning, it looks like there are patches of blue sky. Maybe the weather pattern has broken (like I did last night) and a new season is beginning. So I'm off to enjoy 58 km of cycling a Rail Trail today.

Day Eleven PM

Ignoring the signs.

When I arrived at the beginning of the Rail trail there was a sign that a bridge further down the trail was out of action. I'd already ridden 10km to get to the beginning of the trail - a detail I forgot to factor into my day's total. So now my day looked like a 68 km day, which is close to my current daily quota at present. I stopped and had a snack before starting. Rail Trails are generally non stressful rides so I was looking forward to an easy 58 km. I figured when I got to the closed bridge, I'd just put in my final destination and Kamoot would give me an alternate route. I had life figured out.

The day was glorious. Nice paths, nice weather and then with about 3 km to go to reach Timboon, I struck the closed bridge. So, I didn't panic. I just put 'Timboon' into my phone and waited for recalibration. Unfortunately, the only way to Timboon by road was 19 kms. That's another 1.5 hours given my fatigue levels. I 'beat myself up' for being so disorganized but knew it was a waste of energy so decided I'd enjoy the ride and stay in Timboon instead.

My sister used to work in Timboon and often spoke of a great cafe. So I found the cafe, had a beautiful late lunch and asked if there was a caravan park nearby. There wasn't. My sister had taken me to one of her friend's houses years ago. I wondered if I could find it. My sister was on a cruise in Canada, so I couldn't ask her! Exasperated, I figured it was only 22 kms to Port Campbell so I might as well ride. I was refueled and the waitress said it was an easy ride.

It was! I found a caravan park. The staff were a little grumpy telling me that the weather was changing in a day or so and I'd be caught in storms. Not the most encouraging news I wanted to hear after getting lost and the prospect of climbing the Otways in storms was not what I wanted to contemplate as I went to sleep.

As I ate dinner, I thought how stupid I'd been to ignore the signs of the day. There'd been at least three! Yet each time, I figured I had a better option. I started to doubt my sanity for attempting this ride. My 'executive functioning skills' go out the window when I'm fatigued. So believing I knew better when I was already tired was just pure arrogance.

Yet hindsight is a wonderful thing. Trusting technology had become my way of being. It had always rescued me in the past. So while I can glean some extra tips on planning for next time - check detour beforehand embarking on ride - no catastrophe occurred, just a little more fatigued than usual!

DAY TWELVE

You were never meant to do this alone. Let the kindness of others stitch your strength together.

Day Twelve

One apostle and the role of doubt!

I visited the 12 apostles which are phenomenal natural sculptures. I grew up in a Christian environment so I found myself singing Sunday school songs that taught the names of all 12 disciples. But my mind stopped at Thomas. As I looked at the pillars in the ocean, I wondered, 'Which one was Thomas?' Thomas was often called 'Doubting Thomas' because he had trouble believing life can begin again when all evidence suggests that death is final.

Last night as I had panicked about the length of my ride, I had doubted my capacity. While I received many messages of support one stood out as harsh. I was chastised for doubting. Immediately I wondered what was wrong with me, that I was doubting? So as I stood in front of these apostles I asked what the role of doubt was? Is doubt really a bad thing? I spotted one pillar that had what looked like a keyhole at the top. It sparked my imagination – what is the key to unlocking doubt's potential? I decided that this sculpture was Thomas.

While I am often called brave, courageous and inspiring, I know I'm also capable of incredible stupidity. And sometimes believing in new beginnings seems both impossible and stupid. Yet in the story of Thomas, Thomas asks Jesus for evidence of new life. Surprisingly, Jesus lets him touch his scars. The evidence that death had happened but can be overcome. He wasn't chastised for his doubt.

What had pulled me from my doubt to belief was evidence. I'd made a list of all the rides I had done that had seemed impossible and yet I had conquered – Vietnam, Spain, the Pyrenees in France. All impossible for someone like me. Yet I conquered them all. With evidence I knew I wasn't being stupid but rather my goal was founded in what I call 'evidential faith'.

I have a deep aversion to toxic positivity. The suggestion that if we allow anything negative then we prevent good things from occurring, I believe is false. I believe in positivity, I believe in pushing boundaries but I'm also a realist. Doubt happens! While I was in a state of doubt, friends gathered and became the positive energy I needed to reassess my goal. With evidence plus positive energy I was able to move past being paralysed by fear and moved towards a new way of being.

Doubt can be good. It can keep you safe until one musters the courage to start a new life. Sometimes we need some evidence to make small changes that push us outside our comfort zone to try bigger things.

Magic never happens the same way twice.

Last night (Thursday) as I went to bed, I was a tad stressed about how I was going to make 93 km with a huge elevation. I wanted a magic moment - an 'Emma' moment or a 'Dee' moment like I had in the last few days. But as I rolled over to try to sleep, the thought came, 'Magic never happens the same way twice!' The line is from the movie 'Prince Caspian'.

In the scene, Lucy is fighting some battle and wants Aslan to come. He doesn't come and she has to fight the battle alone. Eventually, Aslan turns up. Lucy asks, 'Why didn't you come like before?' To which he replies, 'Magic never happens the same way twice my dear one!'

So I figured I was going to do this ride on my own. I figured I had the inner resources, and I'd just see how far I could go. I remembered that this time last year I had ridden up a mountain in Spain (1300m) to O Cerebrio. I was at my weakest, yet as the day panned out, it proved an easy ride. I had felt supported by the love of my friends back home. So I went to sleep with the resolve that I can do this.

But I woke in the early hours of the morning and doubt started to creep in. I opened my iPad to check the time - 2:33 (which is my magic number - it means *all will be well*). At the bottom of the screen there were three messages:

One from a woman in Austria, saying she was cheering me on.

Another from a woman in the US saying the same thing.

And then another woman saying 'You'll make it, you've got 15,500 cyclists cheering you on.

I'd joined a 'random' cycling group before I left. I thought it'd be nice to share the journey. The thought of 15,500 cyclists willing me up a hill injected me with enormous energy. I fell asleep content that I'd be fine.

I woke but was concerned where I'd stay if I didn't make the whole distance. The only campsite was Johanna but there was no power. Losing contact with my team makes me nervous. What if I wake and my legs aren't working. I decided I had to make it to Apollo Bay. Then suddenly I got a message from a cycling friend back home. She offered to 'buy me a bed' no matter how far I got.

I felt secure and started my ride feeling confident. I wanted to sightsee along the way but was concerned about making Apollo Bay. I took a turn off to a cafe but when I got up the hill, the cafe wasn't open. So I made a picnic from my stash and enjoyed the view. I saw a guy inspecting Sheeba. I wandered over and he told me he was very impressed by her gears. We chatted for a while and then saw his jacket. On the pocket it said 'Find your own way!' I smiled. Very appropriate. Maybe I didn't have to rush. All would be well. 30 kms went fast.

And then I hit the climbs. I couldn't ride with Sheeba's extra weight. So we walked and rode and walked and rode. Yet each time I got back on my bike my legs grew weaker. Sheeba and I had a near miss at one point. I lost my balance and leaned back on the guard rail. But Sheeba lost her balance too and pinned me to the rail. Her bag got caught under the lip of the rail. I had no idea how we would free ourselves. But we did! So I figured I just had to get to Johanna and text Tas to say I was Ok and just hope my legs were fine in the morning.

'Komoot' took me on a very deserted route. I had no idea where I was. My legs were growing weaker by the minute. When suddenly a little red car appeared. It stopped and the lady asked if I was Ok? If there was anything I needed? She offered to let me take a break at her place. They had a 'shack' a couple of Kms down the road. We put my panniers in her car, so I could ride the 3 kms and drove off. I wondered as she drove away whether that was such a good idea.

I found the house. There was a houseful of guests. My host, Mischy, offered to make me a cup of tea. The other guests asked what I was doing in the middle of nowhere. I told them my story- MS, paralysis etc - Mischy spun around and said, 'I didn't think there was a cure for MS.'

'There isn't!' I replied.

'But look at you, you'd never know.'

'Precisely my point! I'm proof you can live well with MS.'

I soon discovered the two of the men there were medical professionals - one a general Dr at Monash Hospital, the other a medical researcher. The researcher asked, 'Are you part of a research project? Because you should be! Look at you!'

We chatted for ages. He was full of ideas on how to get sponsorship for my big ride.

They let me set up my tent in the backyard. They invited me for drinks and nibbles, for dinner. I soon discovered that the wife of one of the guys was a researcher in 'disability'. Mischa was a sociologist studying the precariousness of financial stability in women.

If there was ever a 'perfect' house I could land in, this was it. They encompassed my three 'Whys' of this ride! And I could go to sleep knowing if my legs misbehaved, medical help was at hand.

The night ended up being magic, conversation, a fire, G&Ts, cheese and bikkies, BBQ steaks, chicken, salad and bread. I went to bed so excited. Why and how does this keep happening?

I couldn't sleep because of the excitement. I put some calming music on in my tent and eventually went to sleep. I got woken in the early hours when an animal tripped on my tent cords. And I couldn't get back to sleep. I went back to the events of the night. How couldn't get any better?

To one side of my tent was the hum of the ocean. On the other, frogs singing in the dam. As I focused on the outside sounds, I was still asking, What else could possibly happen, when a little voice inside my head said 'you could meet a frog?' 🩶

DAY THIRTEEN

When you can't see the whole path, trust the next pedal, the next breath, the next brave yes.

Day Thirteen

A day of total stupidity!

I set off early this morning still excited about the events of yesterday. But it was very short-lived! I'd been told that there are a few more hills and then it was basically a descent to Apollo bay. The hills were steep and the ground very uneven. On the first hill, Sheeba lost her balance and her bag got stuck in a rut. I couldn't lift her. So I dismantled all of her bags and spent the first hour lugging bags, bike and sleeping bag up and down hills, one at a time. I figured I had all day. I only had to do 44 km.

The view from the top was spectacular, but the wind was violent. Every time I'd stand Sheeba up she'd blow over. I eventually found a sheltered spot, loaded her and resolved we would walk down the hill. It was far too risky given my day yesterday. I took a photo of the path and sent it to Tas. His response: I think you're on the wrong bike! (ha ha)

I ran into some hikers walking the opposite direction, some were encouraging, others more scary. I spent the first couple of hours lifting Sheeba over mud puddles, navigating rocky paths. opening and shutting gates and occasionally taking photos. I couldn't let go of Sheeba as she would simply fall over. I made it to Johanna Beach and had 38 km to go but the app said 'expert level required'. 'Surely I've done the expert bit already', I thought. I stood Sheeba on solid concrete and went for a short walk to see the beach. I returned. She had blown over again. 'Can't I leave you for five minutes?' I asked. I heaved her up all fully loaded, grateful for the weight training I'd done prior to my ride.

The road was bitumen so I figured it would be easy from here. A couple of hours and I'd be in Apollo Bay. I was so wrong. The gradient was so steep. Like yesterday, we rode, walked and rode again. But today I couldn't let go of Sheeba at all. The angle of the ground meant she would fall over and I was running low on strength rapidly.

We reached the Great Ocean Road and were immediately confronted with a decline and a long gradual incline. My legs were jelly. So I crossed the road, found a section of flat ground, stood Sheeba up and told her to 'stay'. I grabbed some food and water and propped myself against the signpost. All was well until I went to stand-up. I could no longer feel my legs. I couldn't weight bear at all. Another 'fuck I'm stuck!' moment.

As I sat there, the self narrative became very unhelpful. I thought I was stupid for trying this ride. I shouldn't have tried an unassisted ride. I couldn't ring my team- it was my fault I was in this state. I needed to fix this. All incredibly unhelpful and unhealthy advice! After a while I contemplated ringing an ambulance. It was the only way to get to Apollo Bay, but then I looked at Sheeba. I couldn't leave her out here on her own, so I just had to wait. It wasn't long and I could tentatively stand but I had totally lost my confidence in riding. We walked for a bit but I knew pushing a loaded bike up to 600 metre elevation was not possible, let alone another 30 km.

There was a section that was a gentle descent. We rode and my confidence gradually returned. There was about 10 km of flat road, beautiful scenery and I was super proud we pushed through rather than panic.

But then another mountain. We started okay. I remembered yesterday's 15,500 cyclists willing me up the hill. We can do this, I told Sheeba. But each bend and incline became more difficult and again she just wanted to fall over all the time. I was sure I was near the top but I knew if I sat down there was a good chance I'd not get up again. But I was done. I leaned Sheeba against a guard rail and sat up against the rail with food and water. I couldn't go on, I thought. But then I remembered. Tas had given me some 'emergency gels' before I left. This was my last chance. I crawled to Sheeba, found the gel, and ate it with some more water. I had enough fuel to keep going. It wasn't 100 m and we started our descent. Most of it was gradual and manageable. We swore at a few inclines, but we made it to Apollo Bay by mid afternoon, both of us still totally functional. Tomorrow is raining, but there's no big hills so here's hoping for an easier ride. I do know I have a real bed for the next three nights so that's energizing!

DAY FOURTEEN

The version of you that shows up tired is still worthy.
Still powerful. Still enough.

Day Fourteen AM

Caring for Carers.

The night had been incredibly windy. My little tent stood the test amazingly well. At 1 am there was commotion and noise opposite me. Their tent had 'deconstructed' in the wind. When I finally crawled out of my tent in the morning, Sheeba had fallen over again. While I realised it'd been windy, my comment to her was, 'What is wrong with you?' (I'm sure she cried). I stood her up, put down her stand and let her go. She immediately fell over. I looked at her stand and it was at a strange angle. Not deformed or broken, just different. My first response was, 'You poor thing. All that falling over yesterday was because you're injured'. I then felt bad because I had overloaded her with so much 'stuff'. I had been too demanding of her.

Way back when I first got Sheeba (back in August) I wrote a piece about her stand being akin to the support people with invisible disabilities need. Sometimes we don't need a lot but we do need support. The disability researcher I met the other day at my 'magic house' was studying family carers of those with disability, specifically mental illness. We had chatted about the challenges family carers face. The lack of pay, recognition, pressure etc. I told her a little of my experience.

As I looked at Sheeba's bent stand, I thought about caring for carers and specifically what has happened in my case. Why have family relationships become so broken, twisted?

I think it's twofold. Firstly, we have commodified care to such a point and independence is so valued that we have a tendency to think 'someone else will do it'. I live in a country where paid care is available so I do have formal support. But care is not just the physical act. It's what it represents- that I matter to someone. The absence of informal support taps into the insecurity that I am not valued as a person.

The other reason – historical evidence. I've seen it many times when I worked as a carer in aged care/disability. I'd meet clients and think they were (on average) amazing people. I'd admire their bravery, listen to their conversations and generally had patience with daily challenges of existence. Family members however would speak of their frustration, their impatience and annoying characteristics of their relative. One day it hit me. I had only known these clients in their current state – there was no history, so I could accept them as they are. Yet family members had a lifetime of memories, some good and some a litany of previous hurts. They were carrying a heap of baggage and it was the baggage that was breaking them.

Yesterday as I had to lug bags up and downhills I began to wonder what I could leave behind. How could I lighten this load? But everything was needed. Also Sheeba and the stand were designed to carry the load. It was external weather patterns that tipped Sheeba's stand to breaking point.

I thought about the potential 'external weather patterns' families face when confronted with caring for someone.

1. Financial: we live in a time when we all feel stretched financially. The prospect of adding another person to that load can lead us to breaking point.

2. Grief: seeing a loved one deteriorate, the loss of potential etc, is scary and often needs expert guidance to navigate the way through.

3. Fractured foundations: if the relationship is already fractured before diagnosis it will surely be tested post diagnosis. Some relationships breakdown because it already was broken and patched up with surface solutions but the foundations were already rotting.

In Sheeba's case I know I could take her and her stand to get repaired in a couple of days time. I.e. I could force her into therapy. I just needed to be gentle with her in the meantime and adapt the way we all operate together. However, it's not so easy with people. Forcing people into therapy to fix what's broken is not helpful. It requires mutual consent, desire and effort. And sometimes that just doesn't happen. In those cases, it means walking away and finding new forms of support. And that largely is what has been in my case.

I have an amazing network of support, but family is not part of that network. My family are nice people, they look very normal and contribute to society in many helpful ways. But the long history of fracture, a diagnosis and societal pressures has led to those relationships not being part of my support network. It's sad but understanding the reasons alleviate bitterness and enhances acceptance, compassion, and forgiveness.

Let's talk about frogs!

While we're on the topic of relationships, let's talk about another invisible consequence of a chronic illness diagnosis – finding love.

Frogs have long stood for my desire for a 'significant other' in my life. The symbol of the frog came from the fairytale of kissing a frog who then becomes a prince. I am enough of a 'feminist' to know that the 'knight in shining armour' is an unhelpful archetype but the idea of a significant other is still attractive. Yet in more 'militant' forms of feminism, the desire for or a need for a partner is often frowned upon. Be your own person. You don't need a man (or another) to complete you. While that is true, the companionship of 'someone to do life with 'is often strong.

Yet chronic illness makes that yearning more complicated. The insecurity of *'will someone love me the way that I am'* is strong. It's easy to get into the mindset of 'defective goods' syndrome-it's hard enough for me to live with my symptoms, why would I subject that to anyone else?

Financial burden. Recently, I was part of a conversation with a group of women about what makes a woman attractive. The general consensus was that a financially independent woman was highly attractive. I left the conversation thinking 'what does that say about my prospects?' I wondered what happened to character qualities like resilience, integrity, compassion, empathy and commitment (let alone love).

Since when did relationships become transactional? But the practical reality plays heavily on the mind

It's a topic not openly discussed and I believe many suffer in silence and resign themselves to a solitary life. I love my solitary existence, but that doesn't mean I don't yearn for companionship. But solitude can easily turn into loneliness when it is founded on the belief that I am not lovable because I have a chronic illness.

Self-love is vital for any intimate relationship. The pathway back to self love and the possibility of new love is precarious and because it is largely silent and invisible, the loneliness can be intensified. We buy into the idea, if we don't talk about it, the pain will go away or if I distract myself (by cycling thousands of kilometres or any other noble pastime) then I can still be happy and content. Yet in moments of vulnerability, the desire returns. I know because I'm an expert in distraction. So when I hear a frog sing while I'm out on my rides and I start to think, 'are there any frogs for me?' I push the pedals harder.

In reality, all the insecurities about love, romance and companionship are the same for all humans. It's just intensified for those who navigate the pathway with chronic illness. And it is that fact that gives me hope. Maybe there is a frog out there for but in the meantime, I celebrate the gifts I do have - the friends I share life with as well as the qualities that make me who I am today. I can love me with MS. My friends love me despite MS. And maybe a 'frog' will too.

Drops like stars.

Cate Green

As I packed up my tent, it began to rain. It was only a drizzle so I thought I'd ride into town, grab a coffee and decide whether to ride or wait. I had to get to Anglesea as I had a real bed waiting for me. As I rode into town, the rain grew heavier and I was drowned by the time I arrived at the bakery. I noticed the stares from people as I walked in. 'Is she insane?' the looks said. The 'bakery lady' told me the rain was only till 10 am. So I figured it's only water and continued.

I started out and I knew it looked totally unwise. But I 'knew' the rain would only be temporary. I had only ridden a few kilometres and the sun came out, the road glistened and the scenery was stunning. I watched the puddles beside me along the road. There was still a very slight drizzle and when the raindrops hit the puddle, it looked like diamonds dropping into the puddle as the light caught the droplets. It reminded me of a story I'd heard a long time ago. A man and his family and friends were stuck indoors due to consistent rain. They were frustrated at the grayness of the day. A little girl, a toddler kept going to the window and saying 'stars'. The adults had no idea what she meant. There were no stars. But eventually someone figured it out, each time a raindrop hit the deck, the light shining would make it look like a star. The child saw stars while adults saw darkness. Perspective changes everything.

As I rode into the emerging light, I realised that this was my favourite time and type of day to ride. I don't enjoy totally clear skies with bright sunshine. The risk of heat stroke and dehydration increase. I view excessive positivity the same way. Too much is dangerous. My favourite time is morning just after a storm. The rain is gentle. The sun pushing through the clouds gives an abundance of rainbows (signs of hope), the air is clean (forgiveness) and the grass is greener – everything is brighter (grace). I watched the diamonds hit the puddles. I also realised I was heading east. The road was a deep blue and looked like the ocean and right in front of me was a big bright light, the sun reflected on the road. I was reminded of the Christmas story where the three wisemen follow a star to find the birthplace of Jesus. It seemed unwise for me to leave this morning yet, I now had a star to follow. My final destination is yet unknown but I could follow the light in front of me and that star is easier to see when the conditions are still cloudy and wet from the previous storm.

The day evolved into a magnificent one. I pulled in for morning tea in a random town and met some lovely people and shared more stories. I finished the day having ridden 72 km in total bliss-some hills but nothing unmanageable, no excessive heat, just a 'perfect day' of riding.

Sometimes we just need to start, even if it seems stormy and have faith in 'local wisdom' that all will be well, the storm will pass and life will be beautiful again.

DAY FIFTEEN

You are rewriting what it means to be strong, with softness, presence, and a relentless heart.

Day Fifteen

Learning to trust maps - whatever form they come in.

I'd been spoiled the previous night with a bed, dinner and a spa so I was feeling quite energised at the prospect of riding to Point Lonsdale. However, I didn't want to overdo the day. I use an app called Komoot to plan my rides. A random guy I met on a train months ago told me about it. One of my favourite features is that it will tell me where to go as I ride. My cognitive skills get compromised the tireder I get, so having someone tell me what to do makes life easier (in my optimal state of being, telling me what to do would be very unwelcome).

The other feature I like is that it gives me options for which route I'd like to take based on what kind of bike I'm riding. So while it doesn't know me, it can slightly adjust the route to my skill level. So this morning I flicked through some options and decided on the one with the least elevation.

I needed breakfast first though, so I tried to read the road signs but was bamboozled as I tried to find a bakery. So I asked a local and he pointed me back to where I had just come from and said the cafe was great. It was. I pressed go on my map and headed off. 270 m elevation for the day and

52 kms. But as I headed out of town, I encountered the first hill. Rather than panic I thought, 'maybe all the elevation is at the beginning!' Eventually, the road evened out on the road and the ride became easy. But then Komoot told me to go right and it seemed illogical yet I trusted the map. Travelling alone riding on back roads is a little nerve wracking. Also Komoot got it wrong a few days back going over the Otways. But I was too cognitively exhausted to challenge its decision. As it turned out, the choice was beautiful and wandered through farmland, bush and eventually onto a bike trail. I was led back to the main road and the traffic started to get heavier and the shoulder narrower. I wanted a back road. I came to an intersection with a sign saying Geelong straight ahead and Ocean Grove right. I didn't want to go to Geelong and Ocean Grove seems like a prettier route but I was nervous as I didn't know what was in store if I chose the Ocean Grove route. I had to trust Komoot knew better. But I really didn't want to go to Geelong. So I followed instructions and went straight ahead. It wasn't long until I was on a rail trail that took me all the way to Point Lonsdale. It was such a relaxing ride. No traffic, no wind, no anxiety, just pushing pedals.

Until I was a few kilometres out of Point Lonsdale and my phone, my watch and my battery charger all died at the same time. I was on my own. I had briefly looked at the map at lunch to see where I was heading so I knew the address and vague direction. I ended up doing about 10 km extra as I asked various locals how to get to my destination. Some had no idea, some could get me close and eventually I found someone who got me all the way home.

▶ Cate Green

I arrived at the home of the parents with a friend (i.e. I have never met them.) They showed me to my room. There's a piano exactly the same as mine in the bedroom I'm sleeping in. And the father of my friend has made it his mission to fix Sheeba's stand tomorrow, my rest day.

DAY SIXTEEN

No one sees the wind, but we see its power. Your strength is the same—quiet, invisible, undeniable.

Day Sixteen AM

Learning to trust maps. Part Two

Living beyond right and wrong

My day yesterday made me think about the role maps in my journey of recovery. There's a tendency to think in black-and-white terms and want to know the right way to go. Alternate/complementary forms of medicine are often pitted against the Western medical establishment and you'll get purists from both camps saying theirs is the right way. My journey is somewhere in the middle. My question, when confronted with a choice, is what will bring more life or which is better or best

I have looked into complementary forms of recovery/management which are based in lifestyle choices. Some I've adopted. Others I found (at this point in my journey) exacerbate my propensity to anxiety and therefore not helpful. I also choose Western medicine in the form of infusions because that lessens my anxiety. Neither is right or wrong, but a case of better.

In terms of therapy, the approach is collaborative between my team and I and it's been a steep learning curve. I've learnt new ways of being that have blown my mind. When I learnt to stand, I thought I was doing it well. Yet my physio discovered, I was using my hands to pull myself up rather than my legs. So I had to start again. Similarly with my EP at the gym, I used my arms to lift weights which seemed the obvious choice – but Tom told me it's much more effective to use my legs. The list is massive of things I thought I was doing well yet discovered better ways. None of what I was doing was wrong. I always achieved my desired outcome but there were healthier, stronger choices I could make.

Even during this ride, the route I take, the kilometres I do, has been collaborative. And for me it's been a tad scary. It's easier to acquiesce to the medical experts and hope they get it right. Team Cate is an awesome team. They know me well and will adjust their programs to suit my personality. Yet sometimes I am left to make my own decisions. Twice in this ride that has occurred and both times I have felt uncomfortable. My 'old way of being' was to believe in right and wrong and if I chose badly, I would be judged for a bad decision.

I had spoken to my OT before I headed over to the Otways. She sensed I was on the edge both physically and emotionally so she suggested an alternate route. I didn't like the option. I really wanted to tackle the Great Ocean Road. She left the decision to me and I chose the Great Ocean Road. So when my legs gave out halfway up the mountain, my old mouldy blanket of shame/ blame descended and I felt I couldn't call my team for fear of judgement. I actually know they wouldn't but when ensconced in shame, rationality goes out the window. Fortunately, the issue righted itself and I could continue.

Today, I spoke to Tas to plan my route from here on. He suggested the inland route was the safer option but also walked me through the coastal option. The choice was mine. Again the discomfort was huge. But this time I chose his map – not because he's right, but given his expertise, it's a better option.

And finally local wisdom. We can follow the expert map or the inner guidance of our own soul but there is a third option. That of the locals. When I've gotten lost and the expert map isn't available and my intuition is compromised due to exhaustion or anxiety, I ask the locals. My journey with MS has been the same. When I'm lost in how to manage symptoms, I ask people with MS. Some are seasoned travellers and can offer a tried and tested method. Others are new to the journey, so they can get me partway. It's not right or wrong, it's what's best for me at the time.

There are very few things in life that require a right and wrong choice. Most of the time the better question is what will bring life?

So tomorrow I will start a new route roughly laid out by Tas but the fine details have been left to me. It's a relationship founded on mutual trust. It's the trust factor that's harder than the simple right and wrong. But if you can be brave and learn to trust the experts, yourself and the locals then the life of freedom and adventure awaits.

Day Sixteen PM

A day of rest. Take three.

I think I'm getting the hang of this rest thing. The morning was spent finding a solution for Sheeba's stand. My host for the night (Rob) drove me to 2 bike shops to find replacement but to no avail. Sheeba is evidently quite unique. So we came back home. Rob has some engineering friends so they put their heads together to find a solution. We then went to the workshop and I watched as Sheeba's stand was put in vice and forced back into shape. It was painful to watch, but it resulted in a functional stand. Evidently the stand was not made to withstand such heavy loads and storms after all. So I need to be a lot more discerning where I use the stand and when I lean Sheeba against the wall. (My interpretation: some people are not designed to carry the load of carer. It's not a defect, just a design detail. Therefore easier to let go of expectations of required behaviour)

This afternoon was a short ride into town and I wandered with my camera. Sheeba and I tried a new surface – sand – neither of us liked it, but at least we tried it. I devised a creative mount for my video camera on my bike so we can try that over the next 11 days. And I spent the rest of the day doing mundane stuff like washing. It's been a wonderful day but I'm looking forward to restarting the next chapter tomorrow.

DAY SEVENTEEN

Progress isn't always measured in distance—sometimes it's in how gently you speak to yourself.

Day Seventeen AM

Do you see what I see?

I have a 'dictionary of symbols'. Now before you think I'm weird, I'd like to suggest that we all do! Let me explain: you see something and immediately you are reminded of something else. For example every time I see a lot of stairs, I think of my friend Sil who tackled 7,500 steps in one day. I see chocolate cheesecake and I remember childhood dinner parties that my parents held. A pipe organ equals my dad. We do it all the time. I like to take it one step further and ascribe a meaning to each symbol, rather than just a feeling.

Grey herons have special meaning to me. They symbolise my definition of a successful relationship for me. Herons are largely independent birds but only find a partner to mate with. Now I am NOT saying that all I want in a relationship is sex but rather that the balance between solitude and companionship is a delicate concept that is important to me. Herons tend to turn up in my world either when a relationship has ended or when I'm getting too dreamy about the future. It's like a heron shows up to remind me what works for me and not to compromise just for the sake of a companion. A friend posted a picture of one online the other day and I smiled. It was just after I'd mentioned my desire for a 'frog'. A prompt reminder to keep my balance.

This morning I went for an early morning walk to see if I could find any nice birds to photograph. One of my MS issues is blurred vision which can make photography challenging – I rely on the green grid and hope it's accurate because to me, it's still blurry. Then posting them online is another level of trust. I hope that others see them as in focus. This morning was one of those mornings. It was partially MS related and partially bright sunshine. So I had to trust the green grid as I wandered along the path. I spotted a grey heron. It was close by and I spent ages with her as we wandered along the edge of the waterway together. Again, I was reminded of the balance that is needed in my world.

I found other birds and flowers and had a blissful time keeping my mind focused on watching what was in front of me rather than what might be. But I was also reminded of times when I have been photographing with others. One of my joys of connection is when you find a companion who sees the world as you do. It's fun to traipse through the bush with camera in hand and at the end of the day realise you've taken very similar shots. They're not all the same. Nobody sees the world exactly the same but the occasional spark of connection makes you feel like you belong.

There's another dimension. How I see me and how others see me is often very different. The inner critic in me is harsh so when I hear words like inspiration and brave etc. I've been dismissive and tended to think, if only they knew…

We all see the world differently. Sometimes we are blessed with moments of connection and sometimes we need reminding that there are other ways to see the world. So believing the positive affirmations when I doubt myself is as important as believing in my own worth when others doubt my capabilities. Balance is always the key. It's my foundational belief in all relationships, romantic or otherwise. So maybe my definition of a heron is larger than a 'significant other', it's about keeping a balance between self and other.

DAY EIGHTEEN

You are not the diagnosis. You are the fight, the joy, the fire that rides anyway.

Day Eighteen

Help me mind my own business

Indulgence and being responsible.

The tale of the broken locker.

(I almost don't want to write this because of its vulnerability. So it comes with a warning – the precariousness of female finances)

The original plan for this ride (and next year's) was to gain sponsorship so I could be financially secure, have a support vehicle and person with me whilst focusing on pushing pedals, raising awareness and raising money for MS Plus. Due to the economic climate, businesses were not forthcoming. The standard line of reply I received was, 'what you're doing is amazing but right now we don't have any funds.'

So three weeks before I was scheduled to leave for this ride, I had to make a decision. Will I pull the pin or go ahead? In the last ditch attempt, I set up a GoFundMe page in the hope I could raise enough to at least get my Victorian ride done. It raised some money so I told my team I had enough to ride for a week and that if I ran out of money I'd come home. I'm now at day 18 and all my needs have been met and often beyond my wildest expectations.

But yesterday my brain went places that no mind (especially mine) should go. One of the symptoms I fear most of MS is cognitive fatigue. Physical fatigue I can cope with – I ride, I'm tired, I sleep and repeat. Cognitive fatigue on the other hand impairs my judgement, makes making decisions (even small ones) overwhelming, my mental health deteriorates and I'm prone to catastrophizing. Given my history of depression, nothing scares me more. Sleep and rest doesn't necessarily solve it. I hold on for dear life and wait for the storm to pass.

My fall on the ferry shook me more than I had wanted to acknowledge. Whilst riding into Rye, I'd seen the sign to the Peninsula Hot Springs and my thought was, 'I'd love to go but I can't afford it.' Staying in a bed for the night meant spending more money than I had anticipated. When I arrived at where I was staying, a friend messaged me to tell me that she would shout me a day at the Peninsula Hot Springs to rest and recover. While I was extremely grateful for her generosity, it triggered in me my sense of undeservedness for such generosity. I mentioned my discomfort for resting to some and the common response was you need to rest. My thought was that I can't afford to rest. Each slow day costs more money and I'm fast running out. My mind went down deep rabbit hole collecting a whole lot of negative thoughts along the way, including 'maybe I should just go home and be a responsible adult', 'I shouldn't be a charity case', 'I need to solve this myself', 'I can't rely on others generosity', 'this is too indulgent', etc.

I figured a good night sleep would reset the brain and I would feel better after a day at the spa. I woke early and did feel better but was still played by the thought of 'what's next after this ride?'

When I was having coffee with the Breeze Bandits the other day, somebody asked me what happens after the ride – advocacy or return to business? The simple answer is I don't know. Advocacy doesn't pay and running a business makes me sick. So I had hoped that this ride would give me some clarity on how to make ends meet. But in the haze of cognitive fatigue an answer seemed impossible. Someone else commented on me being an artist – again the thought, 'Art doesn't pay'. So my desperate solution was to go home and get a real job.

I am wise enough to know not to make rash decisions in a cognitive fatigue haze, so I decided to enjoy the day at the spa and then make a rational decision. I arrived and headed off to breakfast. I was early. So I wandered through the gift shop. Instead of seeing beauty, all I could see was what I couldn't afford. Financial failure started to engulf me. I ate the most beautiful breakfast plagued by the guilt that I should be able to pay for it myself. By the time I arrived to get changed, my state of mind was all wrong. I chose a locker and couldn't get the lock to work. I felt foolish for not knowing. I eventually asked a woman nearby, she couldn't work it either. We changed lockers and suddenly I could lock the door. The woman said, 'oh the other one must be broken.' I'm so quick to blame myself for anything that goes wrong.

The first few pools were spent in mental darkness. I desperately wanted to escape the prison I was buried in. So I returned to my why? What's the reason I'm riding? However the answer was phrased like this: 'Am I the only failure of the neo liberal feminist project?' At that point I knew I was so far down the rabbit hole I needed to get out real fast. So I made the decision to 'get out of my head' and go and do what I do well - people watch. It was fun for a bit but eavesdropping on conversations made me realise almost everyone was anxious about something. By the third or fourth pool I was like, 'Why can't people just enjoy the day?' When a little voice inside my head said 'five minutes ago you were trying to solve the sociopolitical systems of your nation'. I laughed at my irrationality. I then remembered my broken locker and my tendency to blame myself for my situation when sometimes the system is broken. I had blamed myself for not being able to lock my locker when in actual fact the locker was broken. So maybe our systems are broken and not me or the others in these pools. But solving that problem was way beyond me so I decided that switching off completely was the best option. So I wandered with Camera in hand and enjoyed the remainder of the day soaking in the ambience and beauty of the space.

I had 21 km to get where I had planned to camp. It was only a 340 metre elevation. I figured it wouldn't be hard but I struggled. Each hill I pushed up, the negativity increased. Each descent I tried to ride, my confidence depleted. Sheeba seemed so heavy – I knew her bags weighed the same but the emotional weight seemed to have doubled the weight. As I headed up one hill, I saw a sign 'Frog Hollow'. Normally I'd laugh. This time: 'Are you kidding? Fuck frogs!' referring to all the poisonous frogs I've kissed in my lifetime.

However I leaned Sheeba against the wall and sat down, rested, ate and drank. Sanity started to return and as I pushed Sheeba up one more hill a song from my childhood returned:

The time has come for you.

You must decide.

What will you do?

Your conscience tells you to

That little voice inside will be your guide

Why would you try to hide from that little voice inside?

Though other folks may disagree.

You can see easily the path that you must walk along so won't you come along?

I believe that this ride has a purpose. It's been my 'why' from the moment I dreamt up the idea. But self doubt is my kryptonite and on days when exhaustion sets in, self doubt is overwhelming.

I finally arrived in Shoreham. My app confidently said, 'you have arrived' but I hadn't. I was at a crossroads, not knowing which way to go (if there was a metaphor there's one). As I began to cry my phone rang. My OT's cheery voice said, 'How are you doing?' I blurted out 'I'm lost and I don't know where to go', when suddenly I spotted a guy (Angel) walking two dogs. I said to Nikki, 'Hang on, I think I found a way.' I spoke with the man, he pointed in the right direction. I had less than a kilometre to go. The camp site looked pretty primitive but at least I had a site. However, I was soon to find that it had everything and more than I needed. I was gifted the night by the managers and provided milk for my tea and coffee. The showers were disability friendly and the best I've had all trip. There was power to charge my phone. The site overlooked the pine forest where my son had married five years ago. The bird life was amazing and the view of the ocean spectacular. I went to bed so content and refreshed and had the best night sleep in my tent.

Perspective changes everything. I can beat myself up for doubting myself or I can be proud of the fact I weathered the storm and waited before making rash decisions.

DAY NINETEEN

When grief visits, meet it with grace. When hope returns, let it stay a little longer.

Day Nineteen

What happens when your companion breaks?

Matching baggage and Mental illness.

This morning I woke up feeling very refreshed. Komoot said I only had 21 km to ride to the ferry and it was classified as easy. I took a leisurely approach to the morning packing up my stuff very methodically, enjoying my porridge and coffee. I checked Sheeba's tyres and they were very under her desired pressure. I realised that may have added to the feeling of overload yesterday, Anyway, I fixed the issue, loaded her up and went to collect my electronics from the bathroom. And when I got there I was greeted by the manager's wife.

'Are you the bike rider?'

'Yes,' and so began a wonderful conversation about my journey, my day yesterday and the magic of the park. She suggested I meet Rosie the Wallaby. We wandered over to the garden that is being built as a cultural space for local indigenous people. I got to feed Rosie, she was gorgeous. But the strawberry was gone in one second. A gardener came over and gave me a banana. Grateful for more food I began to eat it. The Gardener said 'it was for Rosie but if you're hungry you can have it.' 'I can share' I said, so Rosie and I sat and had breakfast together. Absolute magic.

I started off on my ride up some hills and eventually the road flattened out. My confidence had returned and Sheeba seemed happy. About 7 km out I spotted a cafe. It looked classy but I really wanted a real coffee. So I pulled in and was arranging Sheeba into a safe space when the group of guys walked by. 'Are you riding far? 'Not today but I've already done 900 km'. So began the story. They asked if it was a fundraiser and where they could donate. I gave some details and they wandered into the shop. I went to order the coffee. The banana bread looked yummy so I added that. I went to pay when all of a sudden one of the guys I'd spoken to appeared with his phone, put it above the eftpos machine and said 'oh I'll get this for you.' Stunned, I thanked him and went to find a table. 'And I had doubted the universe's provision!' I thought.

Sheeba and I continued and we came to Balnarring. There was a nice village of shops and I was tempted to stop as the wind had begun to pick up. But instead, I decided to take Sheeba along the footpath. It seemed more protected. But we hit a bump going up a ramp. She jolted. As we continued Sheeba was very resistant and there was a very strange noise coming from her wheels. I stopped and spun her front wheel. It was good, nothing seemed out of place on the back wheel. But I don't know much. I got back on and the same resistance and noise continued. I pulled over on some grass, got down on my knees and discovered the pannier rack was bent and rubbing on her tire. So I unloaded all of her bags. The screw holding the rack to the bike was bent. I always tried to match the weight as I've packed so as to not overload her, but the jolt had pushed her over her tolerance level. I bent the rack back and made it level. I reassessed the bag weights but as soon as I loaded one bag the rack came and drifted and the screw fell out. I needed an Allan key. Mine was somewhere but right now I couldn't find them. So I went to the supermarket across the road and bought a set, reassembled the rack to Sheeba's frame, loaded the bag (Sheeba stood by herself the whole time) and we were off again. The last 10 km of the ride I spent thinking about matching baggage. A friend has written the song 'Matching Baggage'. The concept, when looking for a partner, is often we want one with no baggage, but rather the better option is to find one with matching baggage, it evens out the load. It's always made total sense to me.

Also someone asked me the other day if I'd had any bike issues. 'Oh no', I replied. 'Sheeba has been perfect. It's been me that's the issue'. And then today she breaks under pressure.

It reminded me of my last relationship. We had matching baggage and in many ways I believed he was perfect for me. I was the faulty one. But then almost out of nowhere he developed mental health issues and was diagnosed with a disorder. I figured it was solvable. If we worked hard enough all would be well.

But it was not to be and walking away was heartbreaking. When Sheeba and I restarted our journey, post her having a screw loose, I was very aware of her injury. Every bump, pothole, I was cautious and super sensitive to any change in her movements. I realised trust had to be rebuilt. While I wasn't angry with her – external pressure and extra baggage had contributed – there was still an element of cautiousness that she wouldn't survive another round of pressure.

Negotiating relationships when the dynamics change whether that be chronic illness or mental illness is challenging. It requires sensitivity, effort to rebuild trust and a willingness to bend on both parts. In Sheeba's and my case, the relationship was easily restored. In my previous partner, not so. Sometimes the damage is too great. Blame is not helpful. Illness creates havoc to both the individual and ripples out to all relationships. Some relationships survive, others don't. But that doesn't mean new ones can't start. But starting with matching baggage is a great way to make sure the journey together will be a balanced ride.

Waiting for the weather to change.

I rode to the ferry at Stoney Point and saw I just missed it. Yet it turned around within minutes. I saw people disembark. I saw a guy with a bike and panniers. I stopped him and asked about the ride over. He told me that the ride had been cancelled due to bad weather. The next one was in three hours. My eternal optimist self thought, 'it will be fine'. The weather app says the wind will die down by then. A girlfriend rang and we chatted about my day, frogs and stuff. It was a nice distraction from merely waiting. And then I wandered a bit but started to get bored so I took out my journal, some food laid on the grass and had a picnic and I wrote while I waited. Eventually 2 pm came and I walked with Sheeba up the jetty to discover that despite my assessment that the weather was calm, the ferry had been cancelled. I couldn't understand why but figured the expert knew better than me. I had one last chance to get across to Phillip Island at 5:15. I had a real bed waiting for me in

Phillip Island so I really wanted to get across. But this ride is about not panicking. There was a caravan park opposite the jetty so I could stay there if necessary. There was no shop or cafe so food would be an issue but I could last overnight.

I went back to the grass where I had been sitting and turned to find a grey heron in the tree. She looked flustered as she balanced in the wind whilst being introspective. It is a perfect representation of my afternoon.

A ferry came in at four 415. I ran and asked if the 515 would be running. 'Yes, definitely' the ferry driver said. 'How could he be so confident'? I thought, 'the conditions look exactly the same as 2:30.'

So I boarded the ferry (very careful not to trip on steps) Sheeba had to learn how to negotiate stairs. I texted my host in Phillip Island and said I'd ride the 10 km to his place. Earlier in the day I had goaded the wind saying, 'there's nothing you can scare me with now'. As we neared Phillip Island, I noticed a big black cloud overhanging the island, bolts of lightning flashed through the sky. Lesson: Don't challenge the weather.

I messaged my host and asked if he could pick me up. I was a tad scared of lightning. I arrived and conscripted the help of two men to carry my bags as Sheeba and I negotiated more steps.

The sun had gone down and everyone left the pier and Sheeba and I were left to rearrange our luggage. It then started to rain massive drops of rain. We made a run for it. By the end of the pier we were both drowned. I hugged a pine tree to draw on its warmth and shelter as much as I could and waited. Eventually, a little red car turned up. We managed to manipulate Sheeba into the back and drove back to the man's house. Once showered and clothes dry and a hearty meal of rice, curry and wine, all was good in the world again. My host had recently been diagnosed with MS so we spent the night sharing stories of how one navigates early diagnosis. So a real bed food and a new friend ends another day.

One spends a lot of time 'waiting for the weather to change' when living with chronic illness. Some days are good, others, you just have to wait it out. Some days when symptoms are mild you can 'ride in the rain' but there are days, when to the untrained eye, the weather looks fine and others wonder why you're not 'doing anything'. You look fine, they'll say or 'you can ride a bike so why can't you work?' But I'm the captain of my own ship. I've learnt to read the 'undercurrent' of my symptoms and know when it's still dangerous to continue as normal. There are also times when my medical team (those who have intimately studied the weather patterns of MS) will warn me of things that may be lurking ahead that I just can't see or predict.

The invisibility of MS is one of the hardest parts of living with MS. We tend to only believe what we can see. If it looks normal then it must be. To be honest and vulnerable (unmasking) about what I struggle with is difficult. I feel like I'm whingeing. But the reality is if I don't explain, ask for help, I risk sinking my ship and destroying the life I've worked hard to rebuild. Storms can still hit and be unpredictable but as much as I can, I try to protect the life I currently have and sometimes that just involves waiting for the weather to change.

DAY TWENTY

You are proof that healing doesn't mean 'fixed'—it means 'whole in new ways'.

Day Twenty

Cycling paths or Bitumen roads.

Choosing the best surface.

When I put my destination (Wonthaggi) into Komoot last night, it came up with a route that was largely gravel. Gravel riding takes more energy so I tried for a road option but Komoot wouldn't agree. As I left the island this morning, Matt (my host) told me there was a cycling track. Komoot took me along the cycling paths all the way to Wonthaggi. There were a variety of surfaces. Some hills but overall a blissful ride. The weather is nice and never once did I need to negotiate trucks or cars or narrow shoulders. Although the gravel was slightly more difficult, it was so much safer than the road.

It got me thinking about my confidence in learning to walk. Initially, I learned on solid surfaces, concrete, floorboards and carpet. The biggest challenge for me was the transition from one surface to another. Floorboards to carpet and back again was off putting but doable. The greater challenge was outdoors. Concrete to grass to stones was scary. With reduced sensation and reduced to awareness of where my feet are, the risk of falls is increased. However, with practice

I can now climb through the bush, climb over rocks on the beach and feel very secure. Yet there are times that I won't try because the consequences could be detrimental. Out here on my own, safety is paramount.

But I also thought about the surfaces I take Sheeba on. She is built for almost anything but transitioning from one to another gravel to bitumen and back again can be challenging. I need to concentrate.

As I rode the gravel today there were moments when the bitumen looked easier. There were times when the road was flat and the gravel Path ascended and I wanted to go the road route but then I'd catch a glimpse of a beautiful view or a big truck on the road and be grateful I'd chosen the harder route. The rewards are great and it is far safer.

It made me think of accessibility for disabled people. There have been very few caravan parks that have had disability showers with chairs. Sitting in a shower for me means I can ride another 5 to 10 km a day, it's energy saving. But also the gravel rail trail was where I can relax and feel safe. The Dance floor, my physio and EP sessions are where I feel safest. I can be me. I don't need to be on edge that I'm slowing others down. I don't need to 'try to be normal'. I know they will adjust their program to my needs on any given day.

It's not that the path of living with disability doesn't have its challenges. Some days I wish I could travel the faster route on main highways but realise it's both taxing on my system and sometimes dangerous. There are times it's necessary to travel on main roads - there is no disabled route to get to my desired destination, so I prepare as best I can but it is always more taxing on my system.

There are also rewards in travelling with a disability (it's not an easy route). I was out today riding and overwhelmed by the sheer joy of riding. I wouldn't be doing this were it not for being diagnosed with MS. I can honestly say that MS is the best thing that has happened to me. There are elements I loathe and find challenging but I am fitter, stronger, healthier (and nicer) then I've ever been pre-MS. I've gained a perspective on life of what's important and beautiful that I had no view of before. I know more about the human body and its systems and optimal needs than I've ever known. There is a danger to 'romanticise' the journey but today's ride showed the balance between the hard work (gravel surface, hills and occasional barriers) of disability and the rewards of taking the slower route.

I got to Wonthaggi and the weather looked like it was about to turn. I asked someone for directions to a bakery so I could have lunch and assess what's my best option for the afternoon – call it a day or continue. I found the bakery and as I was parking Sheeba, a woman approached me and asked what I was doing. I told her about my ride. She pointed to my tent, 'So you camp?' she questioned. 'I do, but I've been blessed with a number of real beds on the way'.

'Where are you staying tonight'?
'Unknown! It depends on the weather.'
'Well you stay at my place if you like.' she said.

We exchanged numbers and I told her I'd consider her offer over lunch when I checked the weather map. The weather looked ominous so I decided to stay put. I arrived at Kathryn's home, sat down to a cup of tea and the rain bucketed down. I had the most delightful afternoon. We shared so much in common and I learnt lots – she's a family therapist. She went out on a date at night and I tucked myself up in a really warm bed, ate a home-cooked meal of pasta ready for tomorrow's ride. Another day of a real bed, food and a new friend.

I am in awe of the magic of this ride.

DAY TWENTY-ONE

This journey is not about perfection—it's about presence, persistence, and being fully, unapologetically you.

Day Twenty One

A rest day on the bike, stranger danger and some very kissable frogs.

(Female intuition and defying social norms)

I've been told by some that one of my 'adorable' features is my bluntness – I say it as it is. My tolerance of the bullshit factor is zero. I've also been warned that for some, such bluntness and intensity can make some people feel very uncomfortable. So when I meet someone who makes me feel uncomfortable with their bluntness/intensity it reminds me that maybe caution is a better option. If you DO NOT want to know about midlife female sexuality, do not read on.

Yesterday, I stayed with a beautiful woman who opened her home to me, fed me, gave me a bed for the night and filled the afternoon with amazing conversations. However, the intensity/honesty of topics discussed made even me feel a little squeamish at times. At one point we got onto the topic of relationships which led to female sexuality. She said, 'I don't know if I'd want to go down the road of living with someone again. I've got a good vibrator, as every woman should because we have needs. After swallowing my tongue from a TMI moment, (& making a note that maybe I should pack one for my next ride;)) we went on to discuss the social expectations of females and female sexuality. She has a list on her fridge of social norms of female behaviour acknowledging that some of those qualities are amplified by Trauma but generally the list is pretty accepted as normal female qualities. She also mentioned the difference in accepted male sexual behaviour versus female. A man can have sex with multiple women and he is said to be 'sowing his wild oats' whereas a woman does the same and she's called a slut. I know the narrative well having grown up in a very sexually repressive environment.

By the time I left this morning, I was a tad overwhelmed by the intensity (grateful but needed some recharge time). I only had 40 km to ride on a relatively flat route. The road was bitumen and a secondary road so there was not much traffic. Such a ride is relaxing for me – my version of rest on a bike. I decided that today was just a chill ride, push pedals and think of nothing. Just enjoy the day.

First 20 km were amazing. Bitumen back roads through farmland. The air clear, the breeze gentle and partially cloudy. Then all of a sudden Komoot tells me to turn left. It's a gravel road slightly corrugated (do I really need that vibrator?). I saw a really unusual letterbox in the form of a female body. I stopped to photograph it. As I did, I noticed the sky change. The clouds started to look ominous. I looked at Komoot's map and it looked like he wanted me to take me through Bushland. His last attempt wasn't an enjoyable experience. I wanted a known, easy ride today. No stress, no drama, just pushing pedals so I defied Komoot's wishes and turned around to smooth bitumen. I stopped at Inverloch for coffee and waited until the storm to pass. I arrived just as the rain started. As soon as I was inside it poured. 'Wise choice' I thought, 'I am glad I'd listen to my gut and defied Komoot's wishes'.

The whole phenomenon of female intuition has always puzzled me. I've been conditioned in a patriarchal system to ignore it and hence ended up in some very compromised situations. Kathryn and I had discussed the topic last night. Her willingness to invite me back to her place was based on a gut feeling.

As I drank my coffee, I thought of other dimensions of female intuition, especially in 'choosing frogs'. I have long believed my intuition is not to be trusted when choosing a partner. I found it interesting that when I called a friend to tell her I was staying at a strangers house, she suggested that I give her the address for safety reasons. I did but told her I was totally okay. I'm staying in a retirement village with an older woman. What could possibly go wrong?

The night before, Nikki had arranged for me to stay at a friend of hers place. A guy whose wife was away. A man I had never met. Initially it frightened me. My childhood education on the dangers of married men and the evils of seductive sexual women had led me to fear men and fear myself. While I trusted Nikki's judgement, I wasn't so sure of mine. The night had gone well and Matt and I had a great night of conversation and I went to sleep in peace. The next morning when he hugged me goodbye I felt fear rise. Not because the hug was awkward but because it was so nice. Old feelings of shame for feeling pleasure, connection, rose without warning. I recognised it and dismissed it as an outgrown response.

But last night I rang Nikki to ask for help to plan the next few days. The weather was looking unpredictable and I wasn't sure I wanted to ride another two days in the rain. She had another friend she could contact that might be an option. So while she considered that, I came up with my own idea. Matt had offered to come and help me out over the weekend should I get stuck. I texted Matt and asked for help and he was eager to assist. I told Nikki and her response was, 'he's a fabulous human'. Mine though was one of doubt. That hug had been too nice. And Matt had the nicest eyes. Could I be trusted with such a guy? Again I put the idea to rest. 'Old thinking' I thought.

The rain started to get heavier while I drank my coffee, so I thought about booking a motel instead of tenting for the night. Matt was picking me up at Leongatha and driving Sheeba and I to Moe. I found myself getting tied up in knots over 'was I sending the wrong message by getting him to drop me at the motel' etc. Totally frustrated at my stupidity for reverting to female shame for being human, I reminded myself that I have a heap of male friends whom I trust implicitly. Matt was just an additional friend. There was nothing to fear and no shame to feel.

I rode off in the rain. Rain and wind no longer frighten me. You just know that it will eventually pass. As I rode, I wondered whether the men go through the same wrangling as women do when confronted with attraction/connection? I have some exceptional male friends who can handle my awkward questions about such things so I made a note to self - I'll ask them when I get home.

I arrived in Leongatha. The sun was out and I found a cafe to have a drink while I waited for Matt. As I parked Sheeba, a gorgeous specimen of a male walked up and asked what I was doing. He pointed at my tent and said 'so you camp?' It was the exact same conversation I had had the day before with a woman. I went to say, 'oh yes, but occasionally...' and then I stopped mid sentence. Did I really want this guy to offer me a bed for the night?

I diverted the conversation and we chatted for ages about his story: a farmer who moved to town after his wife died and he had a health crisis of his own. He was super friendly and that teenage rush of connection hit me. I could've listened to him for hours. I was glad Matt was coming because this 'frog' was very kissable. We both hesitated as we parted but he wished me well and I suggested he take up cycling. He told me he was very jealous of me, as he walked away with a very cute smile.

As I waited for Matt, I thought about Kathryn's list on the fridge. The social norms that now exist are that men should not be trusted. Stranger danger is what we are taught as women. We live in a state of fear. Yet statistically (and experientially) I'm more likely to be raped to by a man I know than a stranger. But that doesn't mean I trust every man I meet. It's what female intuition is for. I can sense 'sleeze' a long way off. It doesn't mean I can't get it wrong, that's why consent and boundaries are important, but living in constant fear is just not healthy.

By the time Matt arrived I was grateful for the warmth of his hug and company. He dropped me at the motel and hugged me goodbye and wished me well on my ride. He's still a very kissable frog, but just not my kissable frog.

It's days like today that I wonder whether the extremes of feminism have merely mirrored the extremes of misogyny. All humans have the capacity to be loving as well as mongrels. Some we feel a connection with as I did with Kathryn, Matt and the farmer. Some are short-lived, some continue and some deepen overtime. It's a willingness to develop trust in our intuition, and mutual trust that determines whether a kissable frog turns into a prince.

DAY TWENTY-TWO

Sometimes your strongest moments are the quiet ones, where you simply don't give up.

Day Twenty Two

Weather for Ducks!

A directionless day and energy sources.

The weather was meant to be unpredictable so I decided I'd catch the train from Moe to Traralgon. Why fight the wind when you don't have to? But before I left Moe, there was a short rail trail that I thought I'd ride. It was out to a power station. The ride was nice but the station was quite ugly. I got to thinking about 'green energy', the ethics behind it and how complicated the whole debate is around energy sources.

It's also the same in regard to food as energy sources, the ethics behind it and the 'healthiest' choices. Nutrition was a big part of my training and as someone who rarely gets hungry, it was a real challenge to eat enough to fuel my rides. It's taken a lot of effort to 'retrain my brain' to eat enough. The story gets even more complicated if you consider the addition of MS. There's a lot of emphasis in some circles on what sort of food is best for people with MS. Like the 'green energy' issue, the food issue around MS is complicated and widely debated over its effectiveness. The combination of learning to eat more food, the right food for cycling and the 'recommended' food for MS did my head in. So I made an executive choice to focus on small changes rather than be a 'purist' and live in fear that I'm eating the right thing. So while I watched smoke billowing out of the power station, I ate my banana and some jelly babies!

Once I got to Traralgon, the weather was extremely temperamental. I have trouble being 'directionless'. The concept of just wandering around town just to see what I could find seemed a waste of time. I need a purpose. So while I had lunch, I researched my options. I found a reserve that had some wetlands. I rode there, took out my camera, started photographing and then the weather turned nasty. I sat in the shelter freezing and feeling utterly miserable. After a while of feeling sorry for myself, I just watched the ducks. I love ducks. Their colors fascinate me. What struck me while I watched was how much fun they were having. They were totally undeterred by the rain. So I grabbed my camera, stood beside a pillar to protect me from the rain and had fun capturing the birds. I had no plans for accommodation, so when the rain paused, I figured I'd ride to the caravan park and set up my tent. I jumped on my bike and rode for about 15 mins and discovered I wasn't wearing my helmet. So I had to turn around and return to the park. By the time I got there, the weather was exceptionally bitter and I was exhausted and cold. A friend was riding through NSW at the same time as me and had had a bitter night the previous night, so I figured if he could survive the elements, then so could I! I pulled out my sleeping bag, crawled in, laid on the bench. With my black eye, my sleeping bag and loaded bike, I really looked like a homeless woman who'd been the victim of domestic violence. I didn't care. I was warm and I needed sleep.

I started to doze when I received a call from a friend. She was adamant I was not going to spend the night outdoors so she would find me a bed. While I appreciated the offer, all I wanted to do was sleep. I had to wait for an outcome. I don't 'wait' well. But I did and the outcome was I stayed in a stunning home with a baby grand piano, a spa, a cooked meal and an unbelievably comfy bed.

It made me realize how often I opt for the 'lesser' option because I'm impatient and can't envision that I 'deserve' better. This ride has been about envisioning what my future might be like when I get back. It's been difficult to dream large when my default setting has been to 'settle' for hardship. I'm to return home in less than a week and I still feel directionless. I have a dream but absolutely no idea how that may manifest. Today showed me that Ducks can enjoy storms and miracles happen in spite of my willingness to accept 'smallness'.

I won't say I'm comfortable with the idea, but I might just have to trust and wait!

DAY TWENTY-THREE

Even in breakdown, you are building. Even in despair, there is still something sacred.

Day Twenty Three

Missing the perfect shot – the fear of missing out

Today was 70 km of near perfect riding. It started out cold and I got swooped by an aggressive Maggie that actually drew blood (I'm okay but it was the first). I pulled into Heyfield for lunch and found some wetlands. As I parked, I spotted the most beautiful white crane perched on a bridge right in front of me. I willed it to stay while I rummaged through my panniers for my camera. I just got to focus and it flew off (I did get it mid flight but it's not what I wanted). I saw a grey heron fly away as I turned around. I missed it as well. 'Damn' I thought 'I missed that too'. I wandered in the direction it flew in the hope that I'd find it but to no avail. The park was stunning, the weather beautiful. I really wanted to wander but was aware I needed to get to Stratford to set up my tent just in case the weather changed.

I turned to come back and as I crossed the Bridge, I spotted a grey Heron. It'd flown back. It took off and arranged itself for the best photo. And just when I thought it couldn't get any better, it flew even closer and landed on the bridge a few metres from me. I smiled. I thought I missed the perfect shot and yet it came to me.

Having lost all bodily function and got it back has had a profound effect on my psyche. While it makes me appreciate every day and it also propels me into hyperactivity. I need to get as much done in case I lose function again. The 'joy' of living with MS is that you know the possibility always exists. While I try not to live with a constant 'what if', I know that it lurks just below the surface. Like today I was constantly watching the sky trying to predict whether I can relax and enjoy a pause or whether I should keep going. And while watching the weather is wise, when it prevents pleasure in the moment, it becomes unbalanced. It's a difficult balancing act to maintain and one I'm getting better at. It just takes daily practice and relinquishes the fear that something bad might happen if I relax and enjoy the moment.

DAY TWENTY-FOUR

Ride through the ache. On the other side of resistance is revelation.

Day Twenty Four

Harriet the Harey turtle, a black cockatoo and I don't like options.

The day I divorced Komoot (almost).

Part of my 'Why' for my long rides is about personal development. Last year when I rode across Spain, I chose a Black cockatoo as my mascot. A symbol representing the overarching 'meaning' of my ride. Spain was about celebrating escaping a 'Shame based existence'. Although I am very much aware that at the back of my mind is a cage waiting to ensnare me once more. Harriet the Harey Turtle was born to represent my life with MS. I describe my existence as having the mind of a hare and the body of a turtle. Trying to find harmony between the two is a constant challenge. This ride has amplified that, as each day seems to present a variety of unexpected challenges.

I had a really cozy sleep in my tent last night. I'd positioned my tent close to the camp kitchen and amenities so I didn't have to go far. The kitchen was so warm, I was tempted to sleep there. I decided to take the inland route a few days back to be near a train line should my legs decide they've had enough. But I don't appreciate having a choice. The temptation to quit is higher knowing that I have an easy option to get home. Each town I get to, the thought crosses my mind, 'Should I go home?'

This morning I woke up and couldn't feel my legs. I tried to do my stretching exercises- hip bridges- but could lift my hips either. My left arm also felt weird. As I lay in the darkness, I wondered if I really should go home. Is the toll too high? As it was still dark, I figured I'd get some more sleep before I decided. When I awoke, I had some sensation so I figured it would just be a turtle day because I don't really like options. If there was no train, I'd continue! As I crawled out of my tent, a pesky thought floated through my brain, 'What if you had to choose between 2 frogs?'

'It's hard enough to find one', I responded, 'And besides, I'd like a frog to choose me. It'd make life so much easier.' I put the issue to bed and slowly packed up my stuff and headed out.

I found a gorgeous cafe, (The badger and the hare). It had a black cockatoo picture and lots of hares and bird cages. Here I was having a turtle day and arguing with myself that no one would choose me - a cage of shame waiting to lock its door!

The day was beautiful (but cold). I put Komoot to work. I was just going to enjoy the day. I chose 'Komoot' as my partner for this ride for a few reasons. One, he has a live tracking feature which gives me security that my coach back home knows where I am. The other is he gives me options for routes from point a to point b. Normally I don't like options but I wanted to avoid highways and it seemed easier for Komoot to choose an alternative.

The first 27 kms were amazing. The roads were mostly gravel but wide and compacted so easy to ride. The more remote it got, the more nervous I became but I was confident Komoot knew the way. In the middle of nowhere, I ran into a bird watching group. They invited me along their walk, so I joined for a bit. It was fun but I was conscious of the time. I stopped for some snacks. I had 33 km to go. I'd be there in no time. However, Komoot's choice of route was insane. The roads got narrower and more treacherous. Sheeba and I had to negotiate riding through sandy soil. The ride slowed to a snail's pace. Then all of a sudden the trek turned to grass blocked by a pile of logs. I went to guide Sheeba around it only to discover it was a swamp on the other side. I swore at Komoot. I had double checked his route this morning and he had promised me that there was some compacted gravel but mainly roads. In frustration, I ended my 'ride' with him, found another partner who's communication skills could be trusted and continued my ride. Fortunately I only had 27 kms to go but as I was in the middle of nowhere, the majority of the trip was gravel (although nice gravel with pretty scenery).

As I rode away from the swamp I thought of the scene from 'The Princess Bride' where Westley had to survive the trials of the swamp. I smiled at the thought of a man risking life in an effort to win his girl. I like fairytales! But I remembered Komoot's bad communication skills. 'Why are men so hard to understand'? 'Did I really want a 'frog'?'

I laughed at where my brain can go when I'm hungry and tired. When I eventually hit a bitumen road and ate some proper food, sanity returned. I'm happy to continue my relationship with Komoot but with clearer and simpler options and a lot more detailed discussion before we head out.

I set up my tent in Bairnsdale, cooked dinner and thought about going home. The solitude of the ride is turning into loneliness. I'm so close to finishing yet the resolve is weakening. I know I'll regret it if I quit but I do get scared of the ultimate cost (physical and emotional) of finishing it. So I looked at the planned ride for tomorrow (not using Komoot - I need to calm down a bit first), the elevation is mild, it's a rail trail so it should be an easy ride, even if it's slow. So an early night, a body and brain reset and we might just nail the end of this ride. 5 days to go!

DAY TWENTY-FIVE

Today is not about how far you go, but how fully you feel the gift of being here.

Day Twenty Five

Keeping the body in mind.

The day Sheeba and I snapped.

In 2013 I did the subject at uni called 'Keeping the Body in Mind'. Its sole purpose was to contest the Western dualism of mind and body. At the time I struggled with the concept – 'of course they're separate', I thought but overtime my philosophy has changed and often when confronted with an either/or choice, I prefer 'and'. The connection between mind and body is ramped up when one lives with MS. I've discovered there is a very short fuse between my legs and emotional stress. Any overload and I'm likely to wake up paralysed. Therefore I have no tolerance for bullshit.

I was gifted the night at a campsite last night and I was utterly exhausted. I slept well but woke up this morning with a thumping headache and every muscle screaming at me. I opened the tent and the day was stunning. My body wanted to stay in bed or go home. My mind wanted to ride so I wrestled with the either/or dilemma. Who should win? It really was a battle of wills. I had seen two donkeys in the field yesterday. The thought had crossed my mind, 'was I being as stubborn as a donkey? While the answer was Yes, I wondered who the second donkey was. This morning I got my answer. It was my body. I didn't want to fight so I rolled over to get more sleep. It was then I realised I had another choice. The choice of 'And'. I could honour my body's desire for rest and my minds desire to finish the ride. I could just stay put for the day and have a rest day. Although I couldn't really afford it, I knew it was a necessary choice.

With the decision made, I took a leisurely morning and rode Sheeba along the path by the Mitchell River. We stopped at the jetty for a picture and as I gently led Sheeba down the steps she snapped. The screw on her pannier rack had dislodged again. I eventually found it and went to put it back together again, but discovered the screw had actually snapped. Both Sheeba and I had reached our limit. As I had gone to bed, I realised the two things that had broken me on this ride was the weather (uncontrollable on my part) and the luggage (controllable on my part). I tried to think if I could cull anything from my load but everything was necessary. But I really needed to survive the ride with somebody to carry my luggage.

I need support as much as I hate to admit. But right now I have no choice but to continue as is. I tried repairing the rack with cable ties but to no avail. So I found a bike repair shop and for $20 they fixed her. She's even stronger than before. I arranged another night at the caravan park and she only charged me $16. I rode to some wetlands and by the river and we just had a gentle day minus luggage. As a shop owner said to me this morning, I'm taking a mental health day. Both of us felt refreshed.

However, I stopped at the cafe for coffee while she was being repaired. I've spent 30 years in the clothing industry – focusing on body image and how clothes communicate. I often get push back from women saying clothes aren't important. 'I want to be accepted and loved as I am. I want someone to fall in love with my mind'. And while being loved for who we are at our core is important, the way we look can create unnecessary barriers. My logic is why make the connection harder than it already is. It's a classic example of the mind body dualism: ignore the way I look and focus on my mind or the opposite – surface beauty with no depth of character. I prefer 'and'. But on this trip physical appearance is not a priority.

At this stage of my trip, my leggings have holes, my tops have stained, my hair unruly and add to the picture I have a massive bruise down the left side of my face from my fall. Today I added a black peak cap and some thongs. I wandered into a nice looking cafe for a coffee. As I looked for a table, I spotted some nicely dressed women glancing me up and down. I smiled at their judgement. I chose a table by a businessman and as I sat down he pulled his bag closer to him. Again, I smiled. Do I really look that bad? At least I had a shower today and I didn't smell.

Humans are strange creatures. We are wired to be alert to danger and visual cues are the most basic. I look homeless and therefore, I'm considered dangerous. If only they knew! We would like to think we're educated and we wouldn't make such judgements, but I know I do. Just today while at the park I saw a guy on a park bench. My reaction: am I safe? Having been the recipient of judgement in the morning for the way I looked, I was careful not to make judgement of the guy at the park. I don't know his story. He might be just like me and a traveller taking a break from the rigours of daily life.

We instinctively want to feel safe and we do that by visual queues. It's a bodily reaction. But if we stop there and don't think rationally, we may miss an opportunity for meaningful connection. The opposite is also true, someone can look incredibly safe but have incredibly sinister motives. It's not the case of either/or but and. I am looking forward to getting home and wearing some real clothes, but in the meantime I brave the world looking like a homeless woman.

So tomorrow is still uncertain. I'm aiming for the rail trail but a local thought a section was closed for repair and I can't confirm until 9:30am tomorrow. The hope is to get to NowaNowa but I just have to take a day at a time...

DAY TWENTY-SIX

When your body wants to stop, but your heart says keep going—that's where resilience lives.

Day Twenty Six

Falling in love again. No, I haven't met a frog (yet)

The ultimate dance of life.

Sheeba and I left early this morning. We were both feeling energised from our rest day yesterday. I met a young couple from the Netherlands in the camp kitchen last night. They asked about my cycling. I told them a brief overview, aware that English was not their first language. I discovered that the guy was a 'body movement scientist' (exercise physiologist in our language) so he was keen to find out how cycling improves life with MS. I also discovered the girl's mother was diagnosed with MS 3 years ago. It always astounds me the connections that occur on this ride.

Sheeba and I travelled the cycling route for a bit. We crossed the Nicholson and Tambo Rivers – both stunning. Sheeba has a beautiful purr when she's happy on smooth flat surfaces. She sounds like a contented cat (or a Ferrari out on the open road). Today she and I were in sync. It got me thinking about relationships. Sheeba and I were happy again. Komoot and I still have 'trust issues' to work through before we can travel together out on the open road. So I used another app today. I decided taking the rail trail all the way to Orbost was a tad risky. I'd have to stay halfway and there was nowhere to stay and no power and I get nervous being totally alone. So I chose to go to Lakes Entrance. It was to be only 40 km and the first 10 were on the Rail Trail. Because the ride was so easy my mind wandered on the topic of relationships – specifically my relationship with my body. I have a motto that I live by:

> *Running towards something you love is far more energising than running away from something you fear.*

After recovering from my paralysis, I became obsessed with exercise – driven by the fear of waking up paralysed again. But I took up ballroom dancing and fell in love with it. My motivation to stay upright was then powered by love not fear. A far healthier way to live. I actually fell in love with living again. The fear of relapses never goes away, but my life is not propelled by it.

When learning to dance, I discovered a strange phenomenon. MS is caused by the insulation around one's nerves (myelin) disintegrating. The messages between the brain and body then get scrambled. When the system gets inflamed, flareup of symptoms occur and when it calms down, symptoms die down. The danger though is the more flare ups that occur, the greater the chance of irreversible damage and permanently losing function. So far that has not occurred for me. Science is yet to find a way to repair the myelin so lifestyle management is one's best chance of minimising further damage.

It dawned on me today as Sheeba and I were having a 'magic' ride that actually there's nothing wrong with my body. My body is the fittest and strongest it's ever been. What's faulty is the communication system between the brain and body. When the communication system (C.N.S.) fails, my body doesn't work. Overall, my system works okay, but it does have two significant weaknesses – my leg function and a tendency towards anxiety and depression. There are others but these are the two that are the most dramatic.

What I discovered when learning to dance is that the system is more affected between the brain and body than the other way round. One day my dance teacher asked me to move my leg in a certain direction. My foot froze and no amount of willpower would make it move. So Rob got down on his hands and knees and physically moved my foot. Suddenly, my foot 'woke up' and I could 'remember' how to move. The process fascinated me. So today I fell in love with my body again. It's an awesome piece of machinery. My rides are ultimately about restoring how the mind and body communicate with each other. It's about listening to the subtle (and not so subtle) messages my body gives me. It's challenging because often I feel like I'm learning a whole new language. My pain signals are different from normal and I have dedicated a lot of time into educating myself (through therapy) about how my body now communicates. Rides like this one make that investment of time and energy worthwhile.

However, the whole topic of communication in relationships led me down the road of new romantic relationships. I don't ride to 'find frogs', but if one jumped across my path, I'd be open to the idea. The whole concept of dating in Midlife often feels so like it is fraught with the same insecurities of teenagers – 'does he like me?' 'Should I ask him out or do I wait?', 'what if I've read him wrongly?' It seems idiotic, yet with matters of the heart – logic rarely wins. Add to that insecurity, a lifetime of heartache and hurt and the chances of overcoming the barriers of new love can be insurmountable. But just like falling in love with my body again, it occurred by investing time into communication styles.

By the time we get to middle-age, we are likely to have weak spots in our communication systems. Certain words, phrases can trigger 'paralysis' or anxiety and our system shuts down. Just like my dance teacher did, sometimes we just need help to 'move our foot' to restore connection. Communication has to go both ways, but it can overcome weaknesses with practice.

There is the possibility though, that like MS, the past trauma has been so significant that the line of communication becomes irreversibly broken. I'd like to think that all can be healed but realistically, it's unlikely. There is hope. I've seen people 'disabled' by MS achieve amazing things even though parts of their body no longer function due to a broken neural pathway. It takes dedication, a love of life and a willingness to keep learning. So while I have fallen in love with life, with my body again, the question still remains: Is it possible to fall in love with a 'frog' again. Only time will tell.

Three days to go until the end of this ride.

DAY TWENTY SEVEN

Let your joy be just as loud as your pain. You've earned every smile, every mile.

Day Twenty Seven AM

50 shades of Green.

Falling in love with my mind.

(Warning: mental health and suicide)

Yesterday as I rode through Lakes Entrance, I was struck by the multiple shades of green. 'Why do we need so many?' I thought. But it added so much to the landscape, one shade would be boring. I'm sure scientifically there's a reason – sunlight, attraction of fauna, water absorption etc – but initially my response was one of beauty.

My surname is Green. My immediate reaction to observing such diversity was, I feel like I'm Fifty Shades of Green. This ride has evoked such a wide range of emotion from utter Joy to sheer despair and exhaustion. I've often despised my capacity to feel emotion widely and deeply and wished I was more stable. We tend to label those who feel deeply as mentally ill but in actual fact illness occurs when we lose the capacity to regulate them safely (for ourselves and others). Having been through a period of mental illness in my early adult life, it left me with a fear of feeling any emotion. I would get angry for getting depressed, for losing perspective. Why can't I be normal and not get tossed around by emotion?

A spiritual advisor back then gave me a great image to take away the 'shame' of struggling with darkness. He described the mind as a mountain. We create pathways over a lifetime of how we respond to certain situations in our lives. They are known and sometimes lead us to unhealthy places. They become our 'default' setting. Therapy is about creating new pathways. However, when huge storms hit – relationship breakdown, illness diagnosis, financial strain, the deluge of emotion (rain) has to go somewhere so it will also rush down the deepest (default) channel. Such an image helped me accept who I was but not love who I was. My logic was I needed to cover over those pathways, build gates to stop access. But yesterday I saw it differently. I'm always going to feel both positive and negative deeply. And I am not emotionally unstable for doing so. Denying emotion impacts bodily function so merely blocking the pathway is only going to do internal damage to my system. I needed to find ways of healthy creative expression of those emotions that don't destroy me or others.

A few weeks ago, before this ride, I became overwhelmed by emotion and considered suicide as a solution. Frightened (and self shamed) for considering such an option (I know better than that I told myself). I went to my psych with the statement, 'I need to stop going here. Help me not go there'. I was shocked at her response. Her explanation – you will always go there. You have been there before and you'll go there again but you have the tools/strength to navigate your way out. You're still here even after so many close calls.

Resilience isn't about not feeling emotion. Stability is not about not being tossed by the storms of life. Resilience is about creating healthy skills to navigate through the storm. Stability is about a strongly built boat that doesn't capsize and sink when a storm hits. However, mental strength is only part of the dynamic. Some storms are so large that even the strongest minds are battered and broken. Suicide should never be shamed as an option, the size of the storm must be considered. A lifelong illness (chronic or terminal) financial stress, social isolation are all huge storms that need community support to avoid our lives sinking.

I have a number of close friends who know me well – they call me a drama queen but support me through rough patches, knowing that ultimately I'll survive – I am resilient and strong. I just push life to its edges. Other newer friends have expressed their fear of my intensity. They love me but worry incessantly. This trip has had them very worried. But they too know with support I'll figure it out.

I have been guilty of deeming the need for support a sign of instability, a sign of weakness. I'm in a town full of fishing boats. Some go out into the wild blue yonder, to catch fish for us to enjoy. While they use technology available to go at the safest times, there will always be unpredictable weather which they have to navigate back to safety. Their skill set and the integrity of their boat will determine how likely that will be. Similarly I have external compasses and technology (therapists) that are used to determine whether it is safe to explore the wild blue yonder of emotional depth. I have skills (practices/creative outlets) that help me navigate that ocean. The ship I've built has integrity. I have redefined my life as one of the most stable I know. I am proud of who I am.

However, the ocean is unpredictable at times. So I know that sometimes I need assistance to get me back home – it's the nature of life on the ocean. This ride has been blissful on some days and wildly stormy on others. On those stormy days, the assistance I received from both strangers and friends have helped navigate me back to safer waters.

I am not alone adrift in the ocean of emotion. I have networks of support to help me navigate through the ocean. I have 'mainsails' that help me change direction should I need to. I have an anchor of belief systems that help keep me grounded should I need to stay put for a while.

Feeling deeply is part of who I am. I can catch beautiful exotic fish. But it is a risky job and not for everyone. I love my life but I don't want to be out on the ocean full-time. But when I'm out there and the breeze is gentle and the sun is warm, it's the most beautiful place to be. It's only when a massive storm hits and I lose sight of the horizon that I need assistance to regain perspective.

To all of you who have helped me do that on this journey I am extremely grateful.

DAY TWENTY-EIGHT

You are not behind. You are not broken. You are arriving exactly as you are meant to.

Day Twenty Eight AM

Lakes entrance to Orbost

Just a 'mundane' day of riding! 61 km

I stayed in a lovely motel in Lakes Entrance. As I was leaving in the morning, the owner and I were chatting and discovered a mutual connection to a fellow MS person who lives in Vanuatu. Again the connections continue to blow my mind.

I decided to take the main road to NowaNowa as the bike track seems too unstable. Yet the motel owner was concerned the road was too dangerous. Having ridden in a variety of terrains and weather, road conditions are the least of my concern. The climb up was fairly gentle and I arrived at NowaNowa in time for an early lunch. As I sat down, I noticed a guy pull up with a bike (and panniers). He kicked down the stand and it was so sturdy. I commented, 'I was jealous of his stand'. He told me 'it's just a hired E bike'. He came over and sat down and chatted while we ate lunch. He had the nicest eyes, but his overall appearance was one of 'poverty'. I'm always surprised how deeply embedded our visual judgments are.

The conversation centred around making the most of our remaining days - a very interesting guy. He told me of some nice rides/hikes around the area. As I went to leave, he said we should ride together sometime! It's bizarre because I dream of a guy being direct but when it happens, it takes my breath away. He gave me his number and I happily rode away. I took the rail trail from NowaNowa to Orbost – 40 km of gravel, trees, bridges and not much else. I put some music on and just enjoyed the day. An occasional incline but just a beautiful 'mundane' day of riding.

I'd been given the address of the lady who had offered to put me up for the night. I arrived and it didn't look like the home of a little old lady, but soon discovered it was. It was a converted shop, fairly rundown but the bed was comfy and warm and there was a bath. She invited friends around for dinner. She cooked us all the roast and we spent the evening telling stories of our lives.

It's moments like this that I catch myself. On the surface we all looked a bit strange – each of us living on the edges of mainstream society yet each of my new friends were genuine hearts of gold people – generous, warm and real. One woman was a masseuse so gave me some magnesium oil for my legs – liquid gold in my world.

I woke early and my host was cooking bacon and eggs for breakfast. She figured I needed filling up before I left. I only had 40 km to go- a short ride in my books. My host was concerned for me. The road was steep, windy and dangerous in her eyes. I stocked up on some food at the local supermarket and headed out . Again, a blissful ride. Others definitions of steep, winding and dangerous are very different from mine. In comparison to what I've encountered over the last few weeks, this ride was a pleasure. I stopped and enjoyed the atmosphere along the way arriving at my destination by lunchtime – another free bed in a questionable hotel in the middle of nowhere. I had enough energy to keep going but an afternoon relaxing by a creek was too good of an opportunity to pass up, especially when I could sleep in a real bed.

Day Twenty Eight pm

Cicadas and Short-term memory loss.

As I rode along the highway today, the scenery and weather was changing. The days are warmer and the trees look hardier. The sounds are also changing. Instead of frogs, the sounds are of cicadas. The song of a frog is so much nicer than the harshness of a cicada. Initially it was grating and annoying but eventually discovered that the rhythm of their screeching is actually a good rhythm to push pedals - it's even, steady and can get me uphills a tad easier.

It got me thinking of some of the recent conversations I've had with men over the past few days. There have been nice 'frog like' conversations, gentle, caring and easy to listen to. There have however, been some more cicada like conversations. The kind that are patronising and mansplaining. These are the men who, when I tell them of my plans for the next few days, tell me that it's too far, it's steep, there are no resources. I need to plan and prepare more. I'm intrigued by the noise. Usually they're not cyclists and know nothing of my journey thus far. Rather than be combative, I've learnt to be pleasant, listen and then do further research. Most times I've discovered that they are the drama queens and what I've planned is very doable. I arrived at my destination today and got talking to young couple from Tasmania. I told them of my desire to ride around Australia next year. An older guy interjected and wanted to know time dates direction etc. His immediate response: 'You won't be able to do it. I've done it on motorbike and it's just too far'.

If there's anything that riles me, it is someone who doesn't know me telling me what is possible or not. All such a comment does is make me train harder and push pedals further. It's a bit like listening to the cicadas today - their noise provides the rhythm to keep pedalling. No annoyance, no anger, just a determination that I've done my research and I'm capable.

My other aspect of my day involves short-term memory loss – ramification of MS. Whilst in Spain I lost a lot of stuff merely because I lost concentration and forgot where I put things. This trip I've only lost two things – a cap and some sunnies and both involved exhaustion and a break from routine. It's similar in the journey of personal development. I get into the routine of writing, reflecting, observing and remembering to stay positive, grateful, not get anxious etc. But when I'm exhausted and my routine gets interrupted, the new habits of a better life are easily forgotten and lost.

Last night I went to bed rather than writing. I merely fell into bed. But almost immediately I forgot what I've learnt the past four weeks. I started panicking about what happens when I get home, about how lonely I am, about the litany of failures I need to fix. It's so easy to forget. The negativity didn't last long. A brief overview of the 'magic' of this ride reminded me that there's a new way of being. The habits and attitudes I've learnt will take practice to become routine so forgetting is likely to happen. But the more I practice the better I'll become.

My tagline for this whole trip has been 'small change helps!'

It does in reference to money, to physical recovery and most importantly emotional recovery. New attitude/behaviours as possible we just need to be patient and keep practising.

DAY TWENTY-NINE

The journey isn't just what you ride—it's what you release, reclaim, and realise along the way.

Day Twenty Nine

Circadian transformation.

We often use butterflies or even frogs as symbols of transformation - the caterpillar becomes a butterfly, a tadpole becomes a frog. But I saw a different transformation yesterday, one of a cicada leaving behind his shell. When I arrived at the hotel I was staying in, I found the guy running it was very much like a cicada. He was friendly enough but just a bit abrupt for my taste. However, he cooked me a beautiful dinner and I spent the night drinking alcohol and chatting to a group of men also drinking alcohol. My ratio to theirs was a lot smaller.

Travelling alone as a woman always presents interesting challenges. I've yet to discover a female middle-aged cyclist out on the road alone. I'm sure they exist but I haven't discovered any. So if one wants company, one must speak to men without feeling unsafe. I like to say that I can tell a sleaze from an opportunist. Most 'drunk' men I've encountered are opportunists rather than sleazes. My host was a gentleman throughout the evening. Another guy, not an opportunist but became very friendly the more he drank. He was very concerned for my safety out on the road, he was excessive in his praise of what I had achieved. Eventually, I excused myself, his friendliness was a little intense for my liking.

I woke up with a thumping headache. My host had offered to drive me to Cann River where I could catch a bus part of the way. 90 km of hills and trucks was beyond me. We weren't leaving till lunchtime. After some Panadol and a sleep in, my host cooked me eggs for breakfast. We got to talking about his health. He has a chronic illness that leaves him in pain constantly. Yesterday had been a bad day. He had taken some meds overnight and was feeling more 'human' today. He ended up driving me all the way to Genoa. It was easier and quicker than the bus. We had a really nice conversation along the way, he gave me a big hug goodbye and was eager for me to drop by on my 'big ride' next year.

As I rode into Mallacoota, I thought of the difference between my encounter with him when I first arrived and when I left. I had been quick to judge based on his maleness but in actual fact his gruffness was merely a struggle with pain. I thought of the shells I've seen of cicadas in the bush. Pain rather than gender can make us protective – we create a shell to defend against any stress of dealing with life. When we have a good day, we can leave the shell behind. I think we are all capable of being cicada like – defensive when we feel threatened by overwhelming stress be that pain or general living. Such an encounter yesterday made me much more compassionate. By the time I left for my final 23 km I saw the guy in a whole new light. I think we both had left our shells behind.

DAY THIRTY

You did not ride to prove you could. You rode to remember you already are.

Day Thirty

I've arrived!

Making the impossible possible.

By 'societal standards', this ride was supposedly impossible on so many levels. But I can reduce it to three main reasons it was deemed impossible - I'm poor, sick and old! Let me flesh that out a bit.

Poor: I'm a pensioner who spends 80% of that pension on rent alone.

Sick: I have MS and have a history of paralysis and the ever present possibility of being so again.

Old: As a woman, I'm deemed past my use by date for my age. Even last night, someone mentioned that at my age, riding 1500 km was not normal!

Yet, I chose to defy the odds and see how far I could get. With a heap of support, I made the entire journey. I've been overwhelmed by the level of support and generosity of people both here in Australia and across the globe. Who knew that someone who often seems so small, could achieve the impossible.

How I'm getting home.

A friend of a friend put a notice on a local community page asking for help for a lift out of town. I also discovered there is a bus but I'd have to wait till Thursday. I also was desperate and Facebook popped up an ad saying a local church would like to pray for me. So I sent them a message, 'I don't need you to pray for me, but if you could help with transport, I'd be grateful.'

I rode over to a cafe this morning minus Sheeba's pannier bags but my tent and sleeping bag was still attached. A guy sitting out the front of the cafe commented, 'is it harder with the load on your bike?' I was surprised. This is nothing I said. Add panniers and it's a nightmare. We chatted and he gave me his name and number should I need a lift out of town. I had been gifted the cabin for 2 nights so I told him I'd be in touch if I needed help. (He was very frog-like so the temptation to play 'helpless female' was very high)

I rode off to find my cabin. As I was pushing up the hill, a guy walks out of the yard and says, 'Are you Cate'? I asked if he was Dougie. I had a message that a guy called Dougie may be helpful. No, he was Craig. The church had sent a message to him to see if he could help and he'd recognised my bike/windcheater from my profile.

So now I had three potential lifts and a bus. By lunchtime, I decided on the bus. (Although the cafe guy is still a temptation).

I spent the day relaxing, Sheeba and I took some gentle rides around the lakes and generally just chilled. I have another rest day tomorrow, which will involve more sightseeing. I'm going home on Thursday and planning will begin for next year's adventure. I have six months to pray, plan and hope for another miraculous journey – 20,000 kilometres in a year.

DAY THIRTY-ONE

The finish line isn't the end. It's the beginning of knowing you can rise, again and again, no matter how many times you fall.

Day Thirty One Conclusion

Help me mind my own business.

Love will find a way.

1 Corinthians 13:12-13.

For now we see in a mirror dimly, but then face to face; now I know in part, but then I will know fully just as I also have been fully known. But now faith, hope and love abide these three but the greatest of these is love.

When I started this ride, I had three 'Whys'.

1. Personal challenge/celebration of what my body is capable of

2. Raise awareness of the invisibility of MS. Just because I look normal doesn't mean I am devoid of daily challenges.

3. Start a conversation around the financial toll of living with a chronic illness and possible solutions.

I believe I achieved those three outcomes but the ride has actually been so much more. The above quote encapsulates what the ride has meant to me on a personal level. The foundational pillars of my existence have always been faith, hope and love. But often they've not been clear due to looking at them through a fog of illness, anxiety and depression. This ride has 'cleared the air' so to speak and for a moment in time (a month) I've gotten to know so many people and also have been fully known by others. The danger of invisible illness is that it increases one sense of not being seen, heard or believed. I have often felt vulnerable sharing the darker moments of this road for fear of being too negative. Yet I believe vulnerability has the potential for healing connection.

Faith, for me, is no longer a set of prescribed dogmas. I grew up in a Christian environment and while I still hold to the stories of tradition, the mystery that holds all life together is beyond comprehension. The synchronicity of this trip has blown my mind. The constant surprises of connection and timing has astounded me. I cannot simplify them as coincidences – there were just too many. There is something larger than all of us that intends for our greatest good. We cannot control or manipulate it any more than we can control the ocean and her moods. Working with that energy requires practice and surrender. It's a lifelong journey.

Hope, for me, it's about meaning and purpose. Losing my business due to MS (plus Covid) led to a total loss of direction in my life. My business I believed was my calling and I couldn't imagine being anything other than a teacher. This ride was about redefining that Purpose and finding a way to give an expression that both gave life meaning and kept a roof over my head. The former has certainly occurred on this ride. The latter doesn't (as of yet) have concrete form. But I have to hope that it will emerge in time.

Love. Faith and hope have long been the strongest pillars I've learnt to lean on. Love has often been a theory. Something to aspire to feeling and living out. It's not that I have not experienced love in my life. I have but it's often been fleeting. A large part of its fleeting nature has been because I've lived in a cave of shame that's told me I didn't deserve to be loved.

While I didn't find a frog on this ride, I have been overwhelmed by a sense of love on this tour of Victoria. I've wrestled with 'deservedness' the whole ride and fought with Demons that narrate all my failures in the darkness of the night. Yet, the constant daily surprises, affirmations, encouragement, gifts and support has helped slay those Demons.

It's easy to say a cliche like 'love is all you need'. I'd like to think love is the foundation you need on which to build all the other aspects of life – career, money, family and relationships. I still don't know how my daily existence will play out once I'm home, but I'm far more convinced of the power of love now than when I started four weeks ago.

To everyone who has made this ride 'magic', I thank you. My gratitude can't be expressed in words. A few people need a special mention.

Tas – my coach – your constant reassurance along the way has kept me both sane and on the road.

Nikki – my friend and OT – your assistance in calming my nerves, helping with logistics and planning has also made continuing, instead of quitting, possible.

Lynneve, Lou and Marie, your generosity and concern has blown me away. Days when I thought I'd have to come home because of my limitations, I've been blessed by your encouragement, gifts and belief in me. It both humbles and energises me to believe that a life with limitation can be amazing, we just need help.

Tomorrow I return home to my 'real life' but with the resolve to keep practising what I've learnt over the past four weeks. All Will Be Well. Life is simple but never easy. It's scary at times requires hard work and struggle at times. But when founded on a community of love, the reward of a life well lived is worth it.

Love Cate

POSTSCRIPT

A few days of home.

Combating Post Adrenaline Depression

The importance of community (and one more frog)

As I rode into Mallacoota, it was overcast and threatening to rain. I'd stopped on the side of the road for a food break but was very aware of the possibility of the grey clouds of depression gathering – a phenomenon known as 'post adrenaline depression' – the letdown after a huge event. However, I looked at my phone and had a message from a friend asking how I was doing? And acknowledging the anti-climax of ending and its associated emotions. It cheered my heart knowing I was 'normal' and that it was all part of the journey.

As I rode into Mallacoota – tears fell (I was glad it was raining). The loneliness of such an achievement engulfed me. After a shower, food and sleep, my mood levelled out and I could enjoy the two days of rest celebrating what I had achieved. The trip home involved 12 hours of public transport. I met some lovely people along the way but kind of wished that I'd taken up 'cafe guy's' offer of a lift out of town.

Again I was nearing home and feeling very ambivalent about returning. Elements of my life I was eager to resume but the messy part of finding a home and finding somewhere to live for five months seemed daunting and anticlimactic after such an adventure. The clouds of post adrenaline depression gathered and suddenly I received a call from another friend, checking how I was doing given the reality of post adrenaline depression. She encouraged me that it was normal and it would pass. It made my arrival home so much smoother. I spent two days sleeping and generally feeling numb. I just had to wait it out.

Then on Friday night, I received another message. Remember the 'cafe guy' in Mallacoota that had been very frog-like? He messaged me suggesting that the next time I'm in the area we could meet for dinner/coffee. If anything can part the clouds, it's a rainbow of hope.

I attended a dance event on Saturday with some friends – getting into the routine of life here is good for my soul. I told them of the offer of dinner and suggested that maybe I could jump on my bike and ride back. They unanimously decided that it was a bad idea. They didn't want to go through the ordeal of protecting me from murder and kidnap along the way again. So some alternatives were given – I could let this frog swim down the river of life and let him go until I ride through town again in 16 months time. Or I could be brave and ask him to meet me halfway on the banks of the river of life sooner.

It's a dilemma, I'm not sure how to proceed. But in the meantime, I return to the practicality of finding funding, finding temporary accommodation and planning next year's ride. However, returning to a community that cares for me makes the transition from post adrenaline depression to a hope filled future easier to navigate.

The danger of chronic illness diagnosis is you read everything through that lens – every twinge, every mood swing is interpreted as illness related. The nice thing about coming home was being reminded that post adrenaline depression is just part of life. It comes, it goes and life continues. So the only unsure part of my next chapter is when, where and with whom do I have dinner?

WHAT IS MULTIPLE SCLEROSIS?

Multiple sclerosis (MS) is a chronic illness that affects the central nervous system—specifically, the brain and spinal cord. It's an autoimmune condition, which means the body's immune system mistakenly attacks its own tissues. In MS, the immune system targets the protective covering around nerves, called *myelin*. This myelin helps electrical signals travel quickly and smoothly along nerves, so when it's damaged, messages between the brain and the body get disrupted.

These disruptions can lead to a wide range of symptoms. No two people with MS are exactly the same, and symptoms can vary in type, severity, and how often they appear. Some of the most common ones include:

- Fatigue (which can be overwhelming and different from just being tired)
- Numbness or tingling (often isn the face, arms, legs, or fingers)
- Muscle weakness or spasms
- Trouble with coordination or walking

- Blurred or double vision
- Brain fog or problems with memory and concentration
- Dizziness or balance issues
- Pain, including nerve pain
- Bladder or bowel changes

MS is known as an "invisible illness" because a lot of its symptoms—like fatigue, pain, or cognitive issues—can't be seen from the outside. This can sometimes make it hard for others to understand what someone with MS is going through.

TYPES OF MS

There are several types of MS. The most common is **relapsing-remitting MS (RRMS)**, where people have periods of new or worsening symptoms (called relapses) followed by periods of recovery (remission). Another type is **secondary progressive MS (SPMS)**, which often follows RRMS and involves a gradual worsening of symptoms over time. There's also **primary progressive MS (PPMS)**, where symptoms steadily worsen from the beginning without relapses.

WHAT CAUSES MS?

The exact cause of MS isn't known, but researchers believe it's a mix of genetic and environmental factors. Factors such as vitamin D levels, viral infections, and smoking may also play a role. It's more common in women than men, and it's usually diagnosed between the ages of 20 and 40—but it can happen at any age.

LIVING WITH MS

There's currently no cure for MS, but there are treatments that can help slow the progression and manage symptoms. These include disease-modifying therapies (DMTs), which aim to reduce relapses and inflammation in the brain and spinal cord. Many people also benefit from physiotherapy, occupational therapy, counselling, and lifestyle changes like eating well, exercising, and managing stress.

Living with MS can be challenging, but many people go on to live full, rich, and meaningful lives. It's a condition that requires flexibility, strength, and support—but it doesn't define who someone is. Everyone's experience with MS is different, and its symptoms can change over time.

What's most important is understanding, empathy, and listening to the voices of people who live with it every day.